MW01504758

THE
ETERNAL
PURPOSE
OF
MANKIND

DAVID NATALI

rockhousepublishing

charlestown • indiana

Scripture quotations marked (AMPC) are taken from the
Amplified Bible Classic Edition, Copyright © 1954,
1958, 1962, 1964, 1965, 1987 by The Lockman
Foundation. Used by permission.

Scripture quotations marked (NKJV) are taken from the
New King James Version of the Bible. Copyright © 1979,
1980,1982 by Thomas Nelson, Inc. Used by permission.
All rights reserved.

The Eternal Purpose of Mankind
ISBN 978-0-9987761-0-1
Copyright © 2017 by David Natali
PO Box 3626
Carmel, IN 46082

Printed in the United States of America. All rights reserved
under International Copyright Law. Contents and/or cover
may not be reproduced in whole or in part in any form without
the express written consent of the Publisher.

TABLE OF CONTENTS

FOREWORD

David Natali is a man whose love and passion for God is revealed in his pursuit of pure and authentic revelation of the Scripture. Within the pages of this book you will find a fresh presentation of timeless truths encompassing God's plan for man, the origin, operation, and intent of the realm and rule of darkness; in contrast, the authority of the believer, and also valuable keys to nurturing an intimate, fruitful and powerful life in Christ. All of these components are masterfully presented in The Eternal Purpose of Mankind. I know you will be blessed and your life impacted in a positive way as you read.

Marty Blackwelder
Blackwelder Ministries
Broken Arrow, Oklahoma

INTRODUCTION

Faint music is humming from the speakers out on the sales floor. The air is stagnant with the smell of leather and rubber, and not a customer has come in for at least a couple of hours. Here I am, silently rocking in the office chair at a tiny, cluttered desk, covered in papers, pens, display accessories and shoe laces, tucked into a lonely corner of the inventory room. But I'm not alone.

The God of all creation, the great I Am, is here with *me,* the manager of this boring little shoe store, having a conversation.

This was after my wife and I had graduated from Bible School and we were just kind of starting off our life as real adults. I had a lot of time to just sit alone and think, to talk with God. The nature of my job made it easy for me. I had managed two locations of the same store during this period of time, and everyone I met had a unique story and perspective on life. Some of them worked for me, and some of them worked at the neighboring stores in the malls.

In all the downtime, there was a lot of time to talk. Having come fresh out of ministry school, I had a passion to share with people about the Bible. I got a lot of different responses, and a lot of times I just ended up really frustrated. I was challenged with how to share what I had inside of me with such a diverse group of people who all had different opinions and experiences with the subject. Many would just focus on one little part that really bothered them, and it would be hard to get past that one thing. I remember one person who could not get over the thought that an "all-loving God" would send a flood to drown the majority of the human race. No matter how much I would bring up the goodness of God, she was always hung up on that story.

How could I show how *that* story and similar ones fit into the whole scope of things and still stay consistent with the character of a good God? To even begin to start to understand the things of God, I've had to zoom out and look at the BIG picture. I've always thought this way, and it has been helpful for me in understanding all kinds of things that happen in life. It has been an effective way to keep cool-headed and follow wisdom when ministering with people or in raising a family.

When I would talk to my co-workers or neighbors and they would be stuck on a small point of detail, I saw that this was actually a negative thought process. They didn't zoom out and see the big picture on this, the big picture of grace. When my friend couldn't see past the story of Noah, I realized it wasn't even really her fault. There was a need to present a more well-rounded viewpoint of God for people to see and have some why's and how's *actually* answered.

I had lengthy discussions both with people who disagreed or couldn't accept the Bible, and with many believers. At one point, every employee in my store was a student at the main Bible school in the city. The most heated, aggravating debates were with these people. In my frustration a lot of questions cropped up in *me*, and in the quiet time I would debate in my own head. I turned to God and His Word for answers so that *I* could have an answer and not just hit a stalemate with these people, or with myself. The more people I spoke with, the more I found that it was much more than just cold knowledge or information that was needed to have someone actually *hear* what I was trying to say. The truth is that when it comes to God, He is much more than the knowledge and information we have about Him, and any knowledge without purpose is worthless. Again, I would zoom out and look at the big picture. Unless I began to speak directly into hearts and find destiny and purpose, any information I could give to people was meaningless.

In the middle of all of this I discovered a common thread. Regardless of what someone believed, I found time and time again that people did not have an answer as to *why* they existed. The Christians I spoke to did not have a solid answer on why God had created them! I knew within myself that there had to be a common truth to the existence, destiny, and purpose of all of us. I wondered what it would look like if millions of people all saw the same truths together. What would it look like if we *really* knew why we were here? Could this be one reason why people of all belief systems are still depressed and hopeless, sometimes even to the point where it seems better to take their own lives? For years I was taught that people lacked love, and I agreed. I assumed that the remedy was to give more of myself over to this person or to that person and they wouldn't feel so worthless. In the scope of the big picture I discovered a great truth: it was not love alone that these people were missing - *it was purpose.*

The way that we are created and wired requires purpose to unfold *through* loving relationships that help fulfill that purpose.

When I teach on this subject I begin with one question: Why were you created? The most common answer is, "to have a relationship with God." My response is to kindly disagree. *The relationship is the necessity for the purpose.* So then what is the purpose?

Let's go back to that stuffy little shoe store. It was here that I heard the Holy Spirit speak to me concerning our purpose. Out of nowhere He asked me a question that I will never forget, and what followed led me into years of study: "What was Lucifer doing before mankind was created?"

I unearthed truths that I had rarely heard taught. It's my earnest prayer that the Holy Spirit opens hearts and minds to these truths as we journey together into our eternal purpose.

QUESTIONS

CHAPTER ONE

WHAT WAS LUCIFER DOING?

What was Lucifer doing before Adam and Eve were created? Why did God choose to place mankind right where this fallen angel was hanging out? I quickly realized that these were questions most people had a hard time answering. I found out that those who already had their minds made up actually became upset with these questions.

The Holy Spirit led me to 1 Corinthians 2:14 in the *Amplified Bible, Classic Edition...*

> *But the natural, nonspiritual man does not accept or welcome or admit into his heart the gifts and teachings and **revelations of the Spirit of God**, for they are folly (meaningless nonsense) to him; and he is incapable of knowing them (of progressively recognizing, understanding, and becoming better acquainted with them) because they are spiritually discerned and estimated and appreciated.*

How many times do we try to understand the things of God without using our spirits? I needed to be reminded that the average person perceiving these things with only his or her mind would call what I was being shown as nonsense. God began to personally comfort me through the entire second chapter of 1 Corinthians. I knew this revelation would change lives for eternity!

These following passages of Scripture in Ezekiel and Isaiah will continue to be referred to for the entirety of this book. These are the anchors to what God is showing us about our destiny and purpose.

> ### *Ezekiel 28:12-26 (NKJV)*
> **12**
> *"Son of man, take up a lamentation for the king of Tyre, and say to him, 'Thus says the Lord God: "You were the seal of* **perfection**, *Full of* **wisdom** *and perfect in* **beauty**.
> **13**
> *You were in Eden, the garden of God; Every precious stone was your covering: The sardius, topaz, and diamond, Beryl, onyx, and jasper, Sapphire, turquoise, and emerald with gold. The workmanship of your timbrels and pipes Was prepared for you on the day you were created.*
> **14**
> *"You were the* **anointed cherub** *who covers; I established you; You were on the holy mountain of God; You walked back and forth in the midst of fiery stones.*
> **15**
> *You were perfect in your ways from the day you were created, Till iniquity was found in you.*
> **16**
> *"***By the abundance of your trading*** You*

ecame filled with violence within, And you sinned; Therefore I cast you as a profane thing Out of the mountain of God;
And I destroyed you, O covering cherub, From the midst of the fiery stones.
17
"Your heart was lifted up because of your beauty; **You corrupted your wisdom for the sake of your splendor;** *I cast you to the ground, I laid you before kings, That they might gaze at you.*
18
" **You defiled your sanctuaries** *By the multitude of your iniquities,* **By the iniquity of your trading;** *Therefore I brought fire from your midst; It devoured you, And I turned you to ashes upon the earth In the sight of all who saw you.*
19
All who knew you among the peoples are astonished at you; You have become a horror, And shall be no more forever."'"

Another version reads as follows:

Ezekiel 28:12-19 (AMPC)
12
Son of man, take up a lamentation over the king of Tyre and say to him, Thus says the Lord God: You are the full measure and pattern of exactness [giving the finishing touch to all that constitutes completeness], full of wisdom and perfect in beauty.

13

You were in Eden, the garden of God; every precious stone was your covering, the carnelian, topaz, jasper, chrysolite, beryl, onyx, sapphire, carbuncle, and emerald; and your settings and your sockets and engravings were wrought in gold. On the day that you were created they were prepared.

14

You were the anointed cherub that covers with overshadowing [wings], and I set you so. You were upon the holy mountain of God; you walked up and down in the midst of the stones of fire [like the paved work of gleaming sapphire stone upon which the God of Israel walked on Mount Sinai].

15

You were blameless in your ways from the day you were created until iniquity and guilt were found in you.

16

Through the abundance of your commerce you were filled with lawlessness and violence, and you sinned; *therefore I cast you out as a profane thing from the mountain of God and the guardian cherub drove you out from the midst of the stones of fire.*

17

Your heart was proud and lifted up because of your beauty; you corrupted your wisdom for the sake of your splendor. I cast you to the ground; I lay you before kings, that they might gaze at you.

18
You have profaned your sanctuaries by the multitude of your iniquities and the enormity of your guilt, by the unrighteousness of your trade. *Therefore I have brought forth a fire from your midst; it has consumed you, and I have reduced you to ashes upon the earth in the sight of all who looked at you.*
19
All who know you among the people are astonished and appalled at you; you have come to a horrible end and shall never return to being.

The very day that God had asked me that question in the back of the store, I read this passage of Scripture. My eyes were opened and the mystery began to unfold before me.

Lucifer was the *seal of perfection,* full of wisdom, and perfect in beauty. He was favored by God! Who *we* are now as believers in Christ is everything that Lucifer was before he sinned! Lucifer was anointed. Then Jesus was anointed, and now you and I are anointed by the same Holy Spirit. There was a connection between Lucifer and the human race that I had not seen before.

Lucifer was in a garden called Eden, meaning "pleasure" and "paradise." God puts those that He chooses to rule over this planet in a place of paradise. He put Lucifer there, and He had put us there. Lucifer was favored, loved, and cared for.

Lucifer was blameless, or perfect. This implies that Lucifer functioned perfectly by God's rules and within God's parameters. He was an *expert* in the knowledge of what was outside and within God's parameters. This is why he knows how to make something look "right" when it is outside of God's order.

At some point God looked inside of Lucifer and beheld iniquity (sin) and guilt! When Lucifer sinned he felt GUILT, and to this day he continually feels condemnation. This is why the devil pours guilt and condemnation upon believers; he has a lot of it to give.

I came to verse 16 and discovered something I had never heard: "through the abundance of your commerce." It hit me! Lucifer was working very, very hard. It was in this context that Lucifer had sinned. He stepped out of his parameters by unfair trading. That word "trade" means to traffic, or to concentrate one's effort or interest. Lucifer was concentrating all of his effort in some form of unfair trading!

When we read that Lucifer was walking up and down on the holy mountain of God, the original context strongly implies walking up and down *slandering God* to his own subjects on earth, and also to the subjects of God. That made me think. Who is it that Lucifer is ruling over? With whom is Lucifer making unfair trade? I knew from the book of Proverbs that God hates unfair scales and balances (Proverbs 11:1, 20:23). Could that have anything to do with what Lucifer was doing before his fall? The Holy Spirit showed me something in a way I had never seen before, in the first person I heard Lucifer say to his subjects, "You have me, you don't need God."

I kept reading! It said his heart was proud. Why? "Because of YOUR BEAUTY"! That word "beauty" refers to physical beauty, but it also includes the beauty that he had created. I kept seeing a pattern of works versus Grace. It seemed as though Lucifer was working very hard and was puffed up by the beauty of what he was creating. I saw it. Lucifer's heart was lifted up because of his beauty, the brightness (splendor) of his kingdom and his authority. I recalled 1 Timothy 3:6 where Paul tells Timothy that the LOVE of money is the ROOT of all kinds of evil.

In verse 17 of Ezekiel 28 it says, "you corrupted your wisdom for the sake of your splendor." Lucifer lost his wisdom when he believed his splendor, beauty, and success were so great that he didn't need God anymore! Something else stood out to me in verse 18: *"you defiled your sanctuaries."* I looked up the word sanctuaries, and in the original language in this context it means a place that hosts the presence of God. Lucifer defiled the sanctuaries under his care that hosted the presence of God - the place where he worshipped his Creator. *We* are now the living sanctuaries of the presence of God. It is no wonder he tries to defile our bodies and souls.

Matthew 21:12-17 (NKJV)
12
*Then Jesus went into the temple of God and drove out all those who **bought and sold in the temple**, and overturned the tables of the money changers and the seats of those who sold doves.*
13
And He said to them, "It is written, 'My house shall be called a house of prayer,' but you have made it a 'den of thieves.'"
14
Then the blind and the lame came to Him in the temple, and He healed them.
15
But when the chief priests and scribes saw

the wonderful things that He did, and the children crying out in the temple and saying, "Hosanna to the Son of David!" they were indignant

16

and said to Him, "Do You hear what these are saying?" And Jesus said to them, "Yes. Have you never read, 'Out of the mouth of babes and nursing infants You have perfected praise'?"

17

Then He left them and went out of the city to Bethany, and He lodged there.

The Holy Spirit spoke to me and said, "My sanctuaries were always meant for exchange." In a few chapters, I will go into more detail about the exchanges of God. Lucifer fell by *unfair* trade or exchange. This was the beginning of the spirit of the world, or the spirit of Babylon, the world's system. Lucifer exchanged things in his sanctuaries between himself and others instead of between himself and God. In Matthew 21, when Jesus overthrew the tables in the sanctuary, He was filled with a righteous anger, anger against unfair trade and exchange in the sanctuaries of God. He had seen this before when Lucifer had defiled his sanctuaries. He knew of what spirit this was when He saw it in the temple. The amazing part is what happened afterwards. *Righteous* exchanges began to happen in the sanctuary! Several were blind and lame, and their sickness was *exchanged* for God's healing! Jesus immediately established righteous exchanges in the temple and said it shall be called a house of prayer, or worship. Children begin to worship Jesus. Later we will look at how our worship is part of the perfect exchange.

Lucifer was anointed, favored, and blameless. In Christ we are anointed, favored, and blameless by the Blood of Jesus. In verse 19 of Ezekiel 28, it says that Lucifer was brought to ashes upon the earth. In Ezekiel's time, the phrase "to be brought to ashes" speaks of the deepest possible humility. (It is not a reference to his body).

Isaiah 14:12-15 (AMPC)

12

*How have you fallen from heaven, O llight-bringer and daystar, son of the morning! How you have been cut down to the ground, **you who weakened and laid low the nations** [O blasphemous, satanic king of Babylon!]*

13

*And you said in your heart, **I will ascend to heaven;** I will exalt my throne above the stars of God; I will sit upon the mount of assembly in the uttermost north.*

14

I will ascend above the heights of the clouds; I will make myself like the Most High.

15

Yet you shall be brought down to Sheol (Hades), to the innermost recesses of the pit (the region of the dead).

Has Lucifer already had one huge humiliation? Was he already cast down in his rebellion and pride in the sight of the nations over whom he ruled before mankind was upon the earth? He had a throne, and that throne was on this earth. We never see a throne unless there is a king, and a king has subjects. Could we say that Lucifer, by his unfair trade and commerce in the sanctuaries of worship, had already weakened the nations that *he was king over*? I think it is fair to say yes. The same thing Lucifer did to his own subjects in ancient times, he is trying to do to you and me today. He is still trying to weaken the nations of this earth. Is he not already weakening our nations to try to rule again as king through the coming anti-Christ?

One can only give what they get from God. If Lucifer's subjects exchanged what they had with God it would have strengthened them, but they exchanged what they had with Lucifer, and that unrighteous exchange is what weakened the nations.

Am I suggesting a world before *our* world? Yes. Am I suggesting a world before Adam and Eve that contained a human race? No. I do not know who they were, but as we dive further in, we can be certain that the subjects of Lucifer were not made in the image and likeness of God like mankind. Lucifer ruled this planet before he fell. We know from the Scripture that Lucifer had a kingdom, and that kingdom was upon this earth. He had subjects and sanctuaries in which to worship and enjoy the presence of God; there was trade happening and exchange was occurring.

Genesis 1:1-3 (AMPC)
1
In the beginning God (prepared, formed, fashioned, and) created the heavens and the earth.
2
The earth was without form and an empty waste, *and darkness was upon the face of the very great deep. The Spirit of God was*

*moving (hovering, brooding) over the face
of the waters.*
3
*And God said, Let there be light; and there
was light.*

In Genesis 1:1 God created the heavens and the earth. However, in verse 2 the earth is a waste flooded by water. This poses the question: "What happened between verse 1 and verse 2?" That is a fair question! God did not originally create everything under destruction. The Hebrew word is "tohuw," meaning useless, worthless, and destroyed. What was destroyed? The word "earth" in this passage would imply dry land in the original Hebrew, and thus Genesis 1:1 should be read: *"In the beginning God created the heavens and the dry land."* God had originally made dry land. Why is the entire surface of the earth covered with water? Could the covenant of the rainbow that God made with Noah have an even deeper relevance? Were there actually two floods, one in Lucifer's time and one in Noah's?

Jeremiah 4:23-26 (NKJV)
23
**I beheld the earth, and indeed it was
without form, and void;** *And the heavens,
they had no light.*
24
*I beheld the mountains, and indeed they
trembled, And all the hills moved back and
forth.*
25
*I beheld, and indeed there was no man,
And all the birds of the heavens had fled.*
26
I beheld, and indeed the fruitful land was

*a wilderness, And all its cities were broken
down At the presence of the Lord, By His
fierce anger.*

When was the only time the earth was without form and void? The heavens had no light; light had to be spoken back into existence in Genesis 1:3. The book of Isaiah states that the earth was created to be inhabited, and it has been since before mankind. We know that Jeremiah is not referring to the flood that happened in the days of Noah. At that time the heavens had light, and the earth had mankind.

> ### *Ephesians 1:4 (NKJV)*
> *Just as He chose us in Him **before the
> foundation of the world**, that we should
> be holy and without blame before Him in
> love.*

Over three times we see the phrase, "before the foundation of the world." The word "foundation" here means to cast or throw down a system or age. In other words it should read more like this: **"since the overthrow or casting down of the previous world's system."** Wow! It is all throughout the entire Bible, and I had never seen it before! Unless I had heard the voice of the Holy Spirit in the back of that store, I would have never known what Lucifer was doing before mankind was created!

I personally like to picture Lucifer as a kind of meteor that slams back into earth, causing a cataclysmic flood that destroys the entire creation that he had lured into following him into unrighteousness. We don't have much of the details of the past world, but we know that it was there. Jesus said, "I saw Satan fall like lightning to the earth." We know that

Lucifer created evil and subsequently *made himself* into the adversary, the devil.

> ### *1 John 1:5 (NKJV)*
> *This is the message which we have heard from Him and declare to you, **that God is light and in Him is no darkness at all.***

God did not create the devil, His favored angel, Lucifer, chose to step out of his parameters, and the consequence of that is what made him who he now is. There is no evil or darkness in God!

> ### *Luke 10:18-19 (NKJV)*
> ### *18*
> *And He said to them, "I saw Satan fall like lightning from heaven.*
> ### *19*
> ***Behold, I give you the authority*** *to trample on serpents and scorpions, and over all the power of the enemy, and nothing shall by any means hurt you."*

This gives us our first glimpse into the purpose of mankind! Lucifer was sent right back to planet earth after his transgression. Jesus gives mankind insight into Satan's fall, and immediately gives us authority. **They needed to know the history of the devil to have authority over him.**

There were more questions that began to rise up in my spirit. Why would a loving God choose to create the human race immediately following the eviction of Satan from heaven? I think the biggest question for me was "Why did God choose to put us in the very garden, on the very planet that this fallen angel abides in?"

__Genesis 1:26 (AMPC)__
*God said, Let Us (Father, Son, and Holy Spirit) make mankind in Our image, after Our likeness, **and let them have complete authority** over the fish of the sea, the birds of the air, the (tame) beasts, and over all of the earth, and over everything the creeps upon the earth.*

When God made the human race in His own image, that means that our physical bodies were in the same form as God! We looked just like God. The word "likeness" means His character. We were created to look and act just like God! Psalm 139:14 it says that we are fearfully and wonderfully made.

The Father, Son, and Holy Spirit also decided to give the human race complete authority and dominion. This includes mankind having dominion over the sun, moon, and the stars! All three of these were made to exist for this planet.

__James 5:17-18 (NKJV)__
***Elijah was a man with a nature like ours,** and he prayed earnestly that it would not rain; and it did not rain on the land for three years and six month. And he prayed again, and the heavens gave rain, and the earth produced its fruit.*

Could Elijah control the rain by praying with authority? Yes! If you look into the story, Elijah never asked God to stop or start the rain. Elijah spoke to the sky himself and told it exactly what to do by faith. The point is that Elijah was a *human just like any of us*. This type of authority is meant for the whole **human race!** Let's look at another example:

> *Joshua 10:12-13 (NKJV)*
>
> *12*
>
> *Then Joshua spoke to the Lord in the day when the Lord delivered up the Amorites before the children of Israel, **and he said in the sight of Israel: "Sun, stand still over Gibeon; And Moon, in the Valley of Aijalon."***
>
> *13*
>
> ***So the sun stood still, And the moon stopped,** Till the people had revenge Upon their enemies. Is this not written in the Book of Jasher? So the sun stood still in the midst of heaven, and did not hasten to go down for about a whole day.*

The sun and moon obeyed a man. In 2 Kings 20:9-11, the sun caused the shadow to move ten degrees for Isaiah the Prophet of God, a man. This authority was given to the human race, to mankind.

The Trinity looked at one another and said, "Let Us make a brand new species that looks like Us and acts just like Us, and Let's give them authority and dominion over everything on Lucifer's old planet!"

Did you just catch the above paragraph? Read it again. One more time.

> *Psalm 8:3-8 (AMPC)*
>
> *3*
>
> *When I view and consider Your heavens, the work of Your fingers, the moon and the stars, which You have ordained and established,*

4
What is man that You are mindful of him,
and the son of [earthborn] man that You
care for him?
5
Yet You have made him but a little lower
than God [or heavenly beings], and You
have crowned him with glory and honor.
6
You made him to have dominion over the
works of Your hands; You have put all
things under his feet:
7
All sheep and oxen, yes, and the beasts of
the field,
8
The birds of the air, and the fish of the sea,
and whatever passes along the paths of
the seas.

What is this new species that God is mindful of them? The word mindful means to remember continually, visit, dwell, and to keep in merciful view continually! What is the human race that You actually visit them by assuming their nature? What is this new species You care so much about that you would put them second in command over everything?

God created the human race to look like Him and act like Him! The question is, why? **The answer is to completely and fully humiliate the devil!** God duplicated Himself in a brand new species, put them on the very planet on which Lucifer had his throne and kingdom on, and gave this new species full dominion over him! You and I were created by the God of the universe to have authority over Satan and all of the works of Satan! This includes sin, sickness, disease, depression, anxiety, and poverty!

Hebrews 2:5-9 (AMPC)

5
For it was not to angels that God subjected the habitable world of the future, of which we are speaking.

6
It has been solemnly and earnestly said in a certain place, What is man that You are mindful of him, or the son of man that You graciously and helpfully care for and visit and look after him?

7
For some little time You have ranked him lower than and inferior to the angels; You have crowned him with glory and honor and set him over the works of Your hands,

8
*For You have put everything in subjection under his feet. Now in putting everything in subjection to man, **He left nothing outside [of man's] control**. But at present we do not yet see all things subjected to him [man].*

9
But we are able to see Jesus, Who was ranked lower than the angels for a little while, crowned with glory and honor because of His having suffered death, in order that by the grace (unmerited favor) of God [to us sinners] He might experience death for every individual person.

In verse 5 it says, "He did not give this earth to angels." Do you know why? It is because He *took* this earth from angels (Lucifer) and gave it to us! **God put EVERYTHING in subjection to man!** We may not see everything the way we should, but we can see the man Jesus. Jesus shows us how this earth was given to mankind. In 1 John 3:2 it mentions that we will be just like Him, for we will see Him as He really is. It will be revealed. We will be like Jesus.

The human race exists to humiliate angels that have fallen, and command angels who have not. Matthew 25:41 says that hell was originally made for the devil and his angels, not for people! Hell was placed/created in the center of the earth, because it is a humiliation to the one who once ruled this planet. As I said earlier, I believe God used Lucifer to destroy his own kingdom! The first step into understanding our eternal purpose is to recognize that we have been created to fully humiliate the devil as Kings and Queens over him.

CHAPTER TWO

WHY THIS TREE
TO MAKE US FAIL?

I have heard the question asked over and over. If God knew what Adam and Eve would do before they did it, why did He create us to fail? I did what a lot of believers do. I ignored the question in my spirit and chose to blindly believe that it was beyond my grasp. There is a problem that occurs when we choose to handle Scripture this way. People will not know if God is good or bad. They will not know if God's definition of good is different than their own. It creates a heart of doubt, and eventually, a life-style of defeat. The good news is that the real answers are actually mind blowing! They propel each and every one of us into our divine purpose!

__Genesis 2:8-9, 15-17 (NKJV)__
8
The Lord God planted a garden eastward in Eden, and there He put the man whom He had formed.
9
And out of the ground the Lord God made every tree grow that is pleasant to the sight and good for food. The tree of life was also in the midst of the garden, and the tree of the knowledge of good and evil.
15
Then the Lord God took the man and put

*him in the garden of Eden to tend and
keep it.*
16
*And the Lord God commanded the man,
saying, "Of every tree of the garden you
may freely eat;*
17
*but of the tree of the knowledge of good
and evil you shall not eat, for in the day
that you eat of it you shall surely die."*

It looks like God formed the man *before* the garden was planted. This is actually a different Eden than the garden Lucifer had dwelt in. Eden simply means paradise or pleasure; it is not a proper noun. Verse 9 lets us know that BOTH trees (the tree of life and the tree of the knowledge of good and evil) are good for food, which is interesting. Before God tells the man not to eat from a specific tree He tells him to "keep the garden." The word "keep" means to guard or to protect. Who is God telling the man to guard and protect the garden from? Satan, the fallen angel that has been cast back down to the planet he used to rule! We all know Adam and Eve failed to "keep" their authority (or proper domain) in the garden. When this happened, sin entered, and Satan became the pseudo-ruler of the earth.

There were two specific trees named by God. There were two choices. There was one command. The question we all want to know is, why? I have two answers. First, without the choice to choose *against* what God had said, we would not be able to be like Him. God has free CHOICE! Secondly, when they ate, they obtained the knowledge of good *and evil.* Before this moment they only knew GOOD; they only knew God. However, because Lucifer created evil, we NEEDED to understand the difference to truly have dominion over it! **I cannot have full dominion over something I don't even know exists!**

Our Creator knew we would CHOOSE to disobey because of a "tempter," and He let it happen. The first act of man's disobedience was not trusting God in what He had told them. They took it into their own hands. God knew we could not fulfill our PURPOSE unless we would fall and *be redeemed*, unlike the devil and his angels.

Are you catching this? There was and is purpose to everything that God does and everything that He allows. **This is why Jesus was slain "since the fall of Lucifer's world" in the plan for redeemed man to rule planet earth!** From our beginning God allowed the human race to fall (just like Lucifer and angels) so that He could be our Savior, and not the savior of angels!

Those who get glorified with Christ will have been through a process, and through the process they will come out as pure gold. God will not allow another "Lucifer event." We are destined by purpose to take authority and dominion over this planet, but we will be tested to make sure we are not going to hurt God like Lucifer did. That is something to sit, stare, and think about. Not everyone will become gold. Some will not trust God through the process, but this process creates God's Glorious Church!

2 Corinthians 12:9-10 (AMPC)
9
But He said to me, My grace (My favor and loving-kindness and mercy) is enough for you [sufficient against any danger and enables you to bear the trouble manfully]; for My strength and power are made

perfect (fulfilled and completed) and show themselves most effective in [your] weakness. **Therefore, I will all the more gladly glory in my weaknesses and infirmities, that the strength and power of Christ (the Messiah) may rest (yes, may pitch a tent over and dwell) upon me!**
10
So for the sake of Christ, I am well pleased and take pleasure in infirmities, insults, hardships, persecutions, perplexities and distresses; for when I am weak [in human strength], then am I [truly] strong (able, powerful in divine strength).

The strength and power, the glory and anointing of Christ consumes my living space when I am so weak I do not know what to do without Him! Why is this true? Because of Lucifer! God does NOT want us to think we did or made anything good happen apart from Him! This is the process!

1 Peter 1:3-12 (NKJV)
3
Blessed be the God and Father of our Lord Jesus Christ, who according to His abundant mercy has begotten us again to a living hope through the resurrection of Jesus Christ from the dead,
4
to an **inheritance incorruptible and undefiled** *and that does not fade away, reserved in heaven for you,*
5
who are kept by the power of God through

faith for salvation ready to be revealed in the last time.

6

*In this you greatly rejoice, though now for a little while, **if need be, you have been grieved by various trials,***

7

that the genuineness of your faith, being much more precious than gold that perishes, though it is tested by fire, may be found to praise, honor, and glory at the revelation of Jesus Christ,

8

whom having not seen you love. Though now you do not see Him, yet believing, you rejoice with joy inexpressible and full of glory,

9

receiving the end of your faith—the salvation of your souls.

10

Of this salvation the prophets have inquired and searched carefully, who prophesied of the grace that would come to you,

11

*searching what, or what manner of time, the Spirit of Christ who was in them was indicating when He testified beforehand **the sufferings of Christ and the glories that would follow.***

12

To them it was revealed that, not to themselves, but to us they were ministering the things which now have been reported

to you through those who have preached
the gospel to you by the Holy Spirit sent
from heaven—things which angels desire
to look into.

That is a passage that blows my mind! Verse 4 tells us we have an inheritance that is incorruptible or immortal, not subject to decay. It is reserved, which means guarded from injury or loss! I am protected from losing my inheritance which will make me immortal! I find that I always think of X-Men at this point! According to this passage the gold that God sees in us is our FAITH, and that faith/gold goes through fire to burn off the impurities. **The fire that will burn off the impurities is the trials that test our faith.** Notice the phrase, "if need be." God is not putting people through hell on earth because He is God and that's just the way it is! Peter tells us that if we need to learn to trust God more we will go through some fire and some trials to remind us that we cannot do it without Him. In other words, if our pride gets too puffed up and we glory in our success instead of in Him, we may need our faith tested. This is the process of humility. Fire separates all the foreign and impure materials from the gold; fire cannot hurt or change the gold itself!

Verse 11 lets us know that Christ suffered and the Father **glorified Him**, and in the same manner, we suffer in trials for the testing our faith, and the Father **glorifies us!** Peter says that angels want to know about mankind's glorification! This is why angels left their proper domain and laid with women before the flood in Noah's time. They were looking into our race, the human race. Even now angels are being taught by the Church the manifold wisdom of God.

1 Corinthians 4:9 (NKJV)
*For I think that God has **displayed us**, the*

apostles, last, as men condemned to death; for we have been made a spectacle to the world, ***both to angels and to men.***

Romans 8:30 (NKJV)

Moreover whom He predestined, these He also called; whom He called, these He also Justified; and whom He justified, ***these He also glorified***

1 Peter 5:1, 6-7, 10 (NKJV)
5
The elders who are among you I exhort, I who am a fellow elder and a witness of the sufferings of Christ, and also a ***partaker of the glory that will be revealed:***
6
Therefore humble yourselves under the mighty hand of God, that He may exalt you in due time,
7
casting all your care upon Him, for He cares for you.
10
But may the God of all grace, ***who called us to His eternal glory by Christ Jesus, after you have suffered a while, perfect, establish, strengthen, and settle you.***

We are partakers of the glory of God! I love the phrase, "after you have suffered a while." It reminds me that it is only "if need be." **Humility is the answer to going through the process with joy.** Humility promises Grace. Humility will exalt us. Humility is faith and trust in casting our issues to

Christ. Humility gives us more grace to resist the devil. Humility is what Lucifer did not and does not possess.

We asked the question, "Why the tree to have us fail?" It wasn't so we would just fail, but to give us dominion, power, and authority over all of the earth. We fell, just like Lucifer and the angels, *but we are redeemed* by faith through grace. It was and is further humiliation to the devil for us to be redeemed while he has no hope of redemption. We now know evil and can have full dominion over it. We now go through the process to become the pure gold, the Bride of Christ; but the process itself is nothing compared to the glory that is coming!

> *Ephesians 3:8-13 (NKJV)*
> *8*
> *To me, who am less than the least of all the saints, this grace was given, that I should preach among the Gentiles the unsearchable riches of Christ,*
> *9*
> *and to make all see what is the fellowship of the mystery, which from the beginning of the ages has been hidden in God who created all things through Jesus Christ;*
> *10*
> **to the intent that now the manifold wisdom of God might be made known by the church to the principalities and powers in the heavenly places,**
> *11*
> **according to the eternal purpose which He accomplished in Christ Jesus our Lord,**

12
in whom we have boldness and access with
confidence through faith in Him.
13
Therefore I ask that you do not lose heart
at my tribulations for you, which is your
glory.

**"The eternal purpose is to have creations of free
moral agents who have been thoroughly tested
and purged of all possibility of rebellion; so that
God can show the exceeding riches of His grace
toward them in all the ages to come without fear
of eternal rebellions!"**

- Finis Dake

When Adam and Eve sinned, they died; they no longer
had eternal life. Their bodies became mortal; they were no
longer the original creation, but a fallen species. However,
they did not sin ONLY by their own will, but they were
deceived by Lucifer. You and I have not sinned by our own
will either; we have all been deceived by "the god of this world"
since the beginning. In Hebrews 10:26 it states that if one sins
by their own free will only, there can be no redemption for
that creation. The devil CANNOT be redeemed because no
one deceived him!

Lucifer was extremely loved, but he sinned without any
deceiver. Mankind sinned; but God redeemed them back to
righteousness to be like Himself again, humiliating Satan! **Not
only did we take his place, but now the human race
spreads like an infection over the whole earth!** ("Be
fruitful and multiply.")

Mankind, the human race, the Church, the "Body" of Christ is the humiliation of the devil. **In Ephesians (above) Paul says that the eternal purpose of creating mankind was for them to rule and have authority over Satan and all demons!** The devil hates you. The devil hates me. The devil hates a believer and a non-believer. The fact you were born a human has caused the devil to hate you. After Adam and Eve sinned, God told Satan that the seed of the woman (Eve) would crush his head. Satan knew that he would be destroyed by mankind, by this new species, the human race.

Satan's humiliation peaks when *God chooses to become* one of this new species that He created for the purpose of humiliating and destroying all the devil has done and all he has become! In this we can finally see who Jesus truly was and is, and who we are in Him.

CHAPTER THREE

WHY IS GOD NOW A MAN?

__1 John 3:8 (NKJV)__
*For this **PURPOSE** the Son of God was manifested, that He might destroy the works of the devil.*

The Bible makes it perfectly clear why God became a man: to destroy what the devil has done to both God and man. The Father did not give the authority to Himself upon this planet, but to the human race that was formed from this earth.

__Philippians 2:5-9 (AMPC)__
5
*Let this same attitude and purpose and [humble] mind be in you which was in Christ Jesus: [**Let Him be your example in humility:**]*
6
Who, although being essentially one with God and in the form of God [possessing the fullness of the attributes which make God God], did not think this equality with God was a thing to be eagerly grasped or retained,
7
But stripped Himself [of all privileges and

*rightful dignity], so as to assume the guise of a servant (slave), in that **He became like men and was born a human being.***
8
*And after He had appeared in **human form**, He abased and humbled Himself [still further] and carried His obedience to the extreme of death, even the death of the cross!*
9
Therefore [because He stooped so low] God has highly exalted Him and has freely bestowed on Him the name that is above every name,

If we as humans never humble ourselves, which God did by one-third of Himself becoming man and humbling Himself to the Father, we will never see the humiliation that the devil deserves. Jesus, changing Himself into the new species, and dying as that new species is one of the best definitions of humility. Jesus did not retain His splendor, but humbled Himself as fallen/mortal man. This is the opposite of what Ezekiel 28:17 says Lucifer did; he lost his wisdom for the sake of his splendor. Can you catch the contrast?

When Jesus emptied Himself, all of His Godly attributes became void and had no effect. He was no longer equal with God. He went from a spiritual, immortal body to a mortal, human body. He left His authority in heaven and on earth. He left the glory He had with the Father.

This topic of Jesus becoming fully man with a mortal body, and remaining fully man for eternity with a resurrected body, can cause some believers to become frustrated. They think it's blasphemous. However, we cannot even know our purpose unless we understand this point. In Matthew 3:13-17, John the Baptist tries to get Jesus to baptize him, but Jesus wants to be baptized by John. John the Baptist did not realize how human Jesus was, but it was after Jesus was baptized in water and the Holy Spirit had come upon Him that He began His ministry! Jesus had to be baptized in the Holy Spirit just like you and I do to have the power to fulfill our ministries.

Jesus used the gifts of the Spirit noted in 1 Corinthians 12-14. He did ALL of His healing and miracles by the power and gifts of the Holy Spirit! He was not able to heal people because He was Jesus; He was able to heal people because He was a man submitting to the Helper, the Holy Spirit. Jesus as a man without the Holy Spirit could not have healed anyone! In Ephesians it says that when Jesus returned to heaven He left the Gifts of the Spirit to the Church, His Body.

Acts 10:38 (AMPC)
*How **God anointed** and consecrated Jesus of Nazareth **with the [Holy] Spirit** and with strength and ability and power; how He went about **doing good**…and, in particular, curing all who were harassed and oppressed by the power of the devil, for God was with Him*

Only a man, NOT God, needs to be filled with the Holy Spirit and anointed. In James 1:13 it says that God cannot be tempted; however Jesus was tempted! In Matthew we read that Jesus was led by the Holy Spirit to be tempted by the devil in the wilderness! I am not saying that Jesus was and is not God; I am saying He chose to become man for eternity once He humbled Himself. Jesus refused to come to earth as

God; that would have defeated His purpose; that a man would crush Satan's head!

Mark 6:2-6 (NKJV)

2
And when the Sabbath had come, He began to teach in the synagogue. And many hearing Him were astonished, saying, "Where did this Man get these things? And what wisdom is this which is given to Him, that such mighty works are performed by His hands!

3
Is this not the carpenter, the Son of Mary, and brother of James, Joses, Judas, and Simon? And are not His sisters here with us?" So they were offended at Him.

4
But Jesus said to them, "A prophet is not without honor except in his own country, among his own relatives, and in his own house."

5
Now He could do no mighty work there, except that He laid His hands on a few sick people and healed them. 6 And He marveled because of their unbelief. Then He went about the villages in a circuit, teaching.

Was the power of Jesus controlled by the faith of the people? Could Jesus not do what He wanted to do at times? Jesus prayed, "Not My will but Yours be done." Jesus had a different will than the Father. In one story Jesus asks everyone to leave the room so that He can raise a girl from the dead; He had to remove the doubt from the room! Jesus said, "I only say what I hear my Father say." Jesus did not know what to say unless the Father told Him!

There are many believers who assume Jesus performed miracles and healing simply because He was Jesus. This theology limits the Church in accomplishing its eternal purpose! Jesus came as a man and was resurrected with an immortal body to show us what our now and our future looks like in Him! In Matthew 28:18-20 Jesus gives His disciples ALL authority in heaven and on earth and tells them to GO!

John 14:12 (NKJV)
*Most assuredly, I say to you, he who believes in Me, the works that I do he will do and; and **greater works than these he will do,** because I go to my Father.*

Why can you and I do greater works than even Jesus could do once He left? The answer is because when He ascended to Heaven He gave us the Holy Spirit. He sent back to us the same power He Himself used to do the works of the Father on the earth. Jesus is God, but since His natural birth He remains a man as God. The Bible calls Him the first resurrected from the dead. That means I might be the 238,987,345[th] person to be resurrected from the dead, fulfilling the Godhead!

We have this (His) authority in the same way Jesus did for the same PURPOSE! Which is to destroy and humiliate the devil himself and his works. There is an important parallel in the Bible concerning this in the mystery of the symbol of human marriage in correlation with our union to Christ.

Genesis 2:24 (NKJV)
Therefore a man shall leave his father and

*mother and be joined to his wife, and they shall become **one flesh.***

Ephesians 5:22-33 (NKJV)
22
Wives, submit to your own husbands, as to the Lord.
23
For the husband is head of the wife, as also Christ is head of the church; and He is the Savior of the body.
24
Therefore, just as the church is subject to Christ, so let the wives be to their own husbands in everything.
25
Husbands, love your wives, just as Christ also loved the church and gave Himself for her,
26
that He might sanctify and cleanse her with the washing of water by the word,
27
that He might present her to Himself a glorious church, not having spot or wrinkle or any such thing, but that she should be holy and without blemish.
28
So husbands ought to love their own wives as their own bodies; he who loves his wife loves himself.
29
For no one ever hated his own flesh, but nourishes and cherishes it, just as the Lord does the church.

30
For we are members of His body, of His flesh and of His bones.
31
"For this reason a man shall leave his father and mother and be joined to his wife, and the two shall become one flesh."
32
This is a great mystery, but I speak concerning Christ and the church.
33
Nevertheless let each one of you in particular so love his own wife as himself, and let the wife see that she respects her husband.

We, the body of Christ, are of His flesh and His bones, not His Blood. The Bible says "flesh and blood cannot inherit the Kingdom of God." However, flesh and bone can and will inherit the Kingdom of God. Jesus spilled His Blood for all of humanity to redeem them with immortal bodies!

The entire purpose of marriage is to show the UNITY of Jesus and His body. If the body (the Church/humans) is flesh, the head (Christ) must also be flesh. In a couple of chapters we will see that flesh and bone comes from the body of the earth, and the blood as our life source comes from the breath of God. This revelation will be important, but the significance here is the UNITY of the flesh of Jesus and the flesh of man. In the same way Eve was made for Adam and from Adam's flesh, mankind (the Church), was made for Jesus from Jesus' flesh.

Genesis 2:18 (NKJV)
And the Lord God said, "It is not good

that man should be alone; I will make him
a helper comparable to him.*"*

The word helper means suitable intellectually (soul), morally (spirit), and physically (body). It was not good for man to be alone so woman was taken out of man. It was not good for the Trinity to be alone so the Church was created out of Jesus! Suitable also means comparable. In other words, we are made His helpers comparable to God Himself, suitable for Him to carry out His authority through us!

How do we become comparable to God? Through trials that burn away the dross to become His glorious church! Ephesians 1:10 tells us that the Body of Christ becomes ONE in the UNITY of Christ. In other words, the same way we are ONE with Christ is the same way the Trinity is one with each other, by UNITY. The Father, the Son, and the Holy Spirit are three different persons but they are ONE in UNITY! I hope you see how awesome this is! We are grafted into the Trinity by becoming one with Christ! Ephesians 1:20-23 says that the Body is the FULLNESS of the Head. He is incomplete without mankind in authority with Him!

1 Corinthians 6:2-3 (NKJV)
2
Do you not know that the saints will judge the world? *And if the world will be judged by you, are you unworthy to judge the smallest matters?*
3
Do you not know that we shall judge angels? *How much more, things that pertain to this life?*

Jesus came to earth with the PURPOSE of destroying the works of the devil, and to fulfill that PURPOSE He became like us so we would become like Him. The Church is commanded by Jesus to be a living organism, full of ALL the authority in heaven and on earth - ready to heal the sick, raise the dead, cast out devils, heal the brokenhearted, and begin to establish the Kingdom of God here on this earth as it is in heaven!

CHAPTER FOUR

WHAT SPIRIT RULES THIS PLANET?

Lucifer was the "Angel of Light" for planet earth. However, when God said, "Let there be light" over this planet, humiliation began to come quickly for Lucifer. Who is the Light of the World? That's right, it's Jesus! From the beginning of this age we see God's plan to put redeemed man into authority and dominion on this planet through the MAN Jesus! We need to understand the spirit of the devil to take authority over that spirit. The spirit that Lucifer created can look "good." It is the spirit of the world, also known as the spirit of Babylon.

Ezekiel 28:16-18 (AMPC)

16

Through the abundance of your commerce *you were filled with lawlessness and violence, and you sinned; therefore I cast you out as a profane thing from the mountain of God and the guardian cherub drove you out from the midst of the stones of fire.*

17

Your heart was proud and lifted up because of your beauty; you corrupted your wisdom for the sake of your splendor. I cast you to the ground; I lay you before kings, that they might gaze at you.

THE ETERNAL PURPOSE OF MANKIND

18

You have profaned your sanctuaries by the multitude of your iniquities and the enormity of your guilt, by the unrighteousness of your trade. *Therefore I have brought forth a fire from your midst; it has consumed you, and I have reduced you to ashes upon the earth in the sight of all who looked at you.*

What was Lucifer trading? We discussed how Satan had already weakened the nations in the sanctuaries of worship by unfair trade and commerce. I had mentioned previously that in 1 Timothy 6:10 it is written that the *love* of money is the root of all kinds of evil! I began to notice that evil was created out of a heart for the love of money or possessions, a heart of covetousness. The Holy Spirit began to reveal that there is a difference between an "even exchange" of what each had (or has), versus making a profit off of deceitful or unfair trade.

As Lucifer began to practice unfair trade, he began to feel that success and profit was created by *his* HARD WORK, and that he no longer needed his Creator. It produced a thought of being self-sufficient. I believe his pride led him into the continual thinking that he no longer needed God. His own efforts provided him with enough, and he no longer saw God the same as when he didn't have as much. Are you catching this? The love of money, possessions, and success changed Lucifer. It created evil. It created selfishness, greed, and jealousy.

John 8:44 asserts that Satan is the father of all of those who do not believe in the man Jesus. John talks about the characteristics of Satan, how he is a murderer, he speaks falsehoods, he is the father of all lies. This sounds like a movie to me. Lucifer was lying and killing, scheming and hiding things to create a world where *he* was the supplier. In 2 Corinthians 4:4 Paul says that Satan is the "god of this world" to all who do not believe in Jesus. Later John says that the whole world lies under the sway or influence of the devil, "the wicked one." *The spirit of the world is the spirit that Lucifer created.* If we do not believe in Jesus who gives light to our eternal purpose, we are influenced by this spirit!

> ### *2 Corinthians 11:14-15 (AMPC)*
> *14*
> *And it is no wonder, for Satan himself masquerades as an angel of light;*
> *15*
> *So it is not surprising if his servants also masquerade as ministers of righteousness. [But] their end will correspond with their deeds.*

The end of Satan and all who follow his system are judged according to their deeds or works. Why? Because they are caught up in working and hustling for success and do not receive Grace (Jesus) to empower them into their eternal purpose!

First Timothy 4:1-2 says that people will give attention and heed (be in submission) to demonic spirits, who through empty philosophy will teach the people that their substance is not in Christ. These demons were the angels that served with Lucifer on this planet way before we were created! They know the system. They use a system of darkness and deceive people into thinking it's a system of light.

One of the first places we see this spirit manifest is at the Tower of Babel (the beginning of Babylon). Do you remember the story? All peoples from all over the earth gathered together to accomplish one goal. At this time all of mankind spoke the same language and dialect. There was nothing to hinder good communication! They believed in the FREEDOM to do whatever they wanted to do, and in that freedom they began to create a city and a tower toward heaven. History tells us that at the top of the tower there would have been symbols of pagan worship; they had already forgotten who God was. They had the ability to succeed, to become what they wanted by unity and HARD WORK! We know that God came down and confused their language to hinder their communication. God was not pleased with the spirit of man-made success without Himself getting the glory.

> ### *1 Corinthians 2:12 (NKJV)*
> *Now we have received, not the spirit of the world, but the Spirit who is from God, that we might **know the things that have been freely given to us by God.***

The above verse gives us the definition of the spirit of the world. It's to KNOW the things that are NOT freely given to us. Grace (Jesus) gives us all things freely. The spirit of the world does not know Grace, it does not know Jesus. It's an "I did it" spirit. In the world we work hard to be the best, however, in Christ we work hard because we are the best.

> ### *Luke 6:30-34 (AMPC)*
> *30*
> *Give away to everyone who begs of you [who is in want of necessities], and of him who takes away from you your goods, do not demand or require them back again.*
> *31*
> *And as you would like and desire that men*

would do to you, do exactly so to them.
32
If you [merely] love those who love you,
what quality of credit and thanks is that
to you? For even the [very] sinners love
their lovers (those who love them).
33
And if you are kind and good and do favors
to and benefit those who are kind and good
and do favors to and benefit you, what
quality of credit and thanks is that to you?
For even the preeminently sinful do the
same.
34
And if you lend money at interest to those
from whom you hope to receive, what
quality of credit and thanks is that to
you? Even notorious sinners lend money
at interest to sinners, so as to recover as
much again.

This passage in Luke realigns my heart every time I read it. The part in bold is saying something most people do not talk about too much. If I gave you $100, and you agree to pay me back when you get paid, then the world would say that I'm a good man. After all, you're the one lacking and I'm the one who has it. However, Jesus taught that **lending** was a practice of the world's system, or demonic. In Romans 13:8 Paul tells us to owe nothing to anyone except to love them. Paul is saying we owe love to every person, but do not take anything from someone who is expecting something back in return, especially with interest! The spirit of the world is about giving (lending) and expecting the same or even more back in return!

I have seen this spirit at its best, and I bet you have, too. This spirit is influencing people to see how much they can get out of a single transaction. People will end up lying and manipulating and twisting anything to make a profit or climb up the ladder (the tower of Babel) to their own personal heaven. They will try to exalt their throne above the clouds without the help of God, just like Lucifer. This is a selfish spirit. This spirit scares people into thinking they will get ripped off, so even some believers stand up against other believers to protect what they have worked so hard to get. When people choose to submit to this spirit long enough, they quickly stop caring whether or not they hurt and abuse others to gain more and more. Do you see this?

When people (under the influence of this spirit) have more, they do not feel the obligation to give what they have worked so hard for to the poor (those with less than themselves). We might think that those more poor than us MUST have not worked as hard as us, and this justifies NOT giving to them. There is absolutely no faith in people who think like this. We are to give to those in need, to those whom the Holy Spirit tells us to give to, and expect nothing in return from them.

I was teaching along these lines one night and afterwards someone came up to me and showed me Proverbs 19:17. It says when you give to the poor you LEND to God! This is the only verse in the Bible that explains how a believer should lend - by giving to the poor. However, we are not lending to the poor but to God, because He gave us the authority on this earth along with its riches! It is His heart to supply to those who lack. We lend to Him by giving what He has given us, and He repays us with interest (so we can give even more)! Look up Proverbs 14:31, 21:13, and 28:27 for more details along these lines.

I did a study on Proverbs once. I pulled out ten main points that Solomon said were wisdom. I found that the fourth wisest command was to give to the poor. It was not just to give in general, but to give to those with less than you! Does giving to the poor have anything to do with what they do with what you give? **No.** Does giving to the poor have anything to do with how they initially got poor or why they are staying poor? **No!** To choose to give to only some of the poor and not others would insult the Spirit of Grace!

I love Matthew 25:33-40. This is the passage where Jesus talks about dividing the sheep from the goats. Both the sheep and the goats seem confused as to whether they are actually sheep or goats! This is where the sheep fed the hungry, gave water to the thirsty, clothed the naked, visited the sick and those in prison, and were kind when Jesus was a stranger to them. The sheep ask, "When did we do this?" Jesus replies, "To the least of these you have done to Me". Then the goats get upset because they would have done those things for Jesus, too, had they known it would have been unto Him. But since they didn't realize that everyone they met was meant to be a part of Christ's Body, they refused. The goats get cast away into outer darkness.

If we were to relate this story to modern times it might sound a little bit different. Did we make someone feel welcome and loved when they weren't in our clique or had different opinions than us? Did we visit and comfort those who were sick from drinking their whole lives? Did we visit the person in prison who stole from us or murdered our brother? Did we refuse to give clothes and food to those standing at the corner holding a sign because we thought they would buy alcohol and drugs? What we have done for the least of these we have done for Christ! The least of these do not always have good intentions and a pure heart. (1 John 3:17-19, 1 Timothy 6:17-19)

Today our country, our culture, our world, and our churches have submitted to the spirit of Satan in varying degrees. Our culture and our country are proud of the success it has had in trade and commerce. We fight and step on people by doing the best we can do to succeed. When we "arrive" we even fight in our politics so that the poor cannot have a chance for government handouts because we are so PROUD of the hard work we've put into getting what we have. In Christ there are neither Democrats nor Republicans. We are not the judge of the world at this present moment. However, some Christians are screaming, "To hell with the poor! They just didn't have the same *work ethic* as us!"

The feeling that 'we have arrived' overwhelmed this country to the point that we took God (prayer and the Bible) out of our education system! This means that we did not want our children to learn how to pray or learn the Word of God. We had arrived at a place of success, in part by unfair trade and commerce, and we thought that we no longer needed God! Even in our churches, we buy our favorite teachers and sell the spirit of the world to a target audience. We have arrived. Does this sound like Lucifer?

Revelation 3:15-18 (AMPC)
15

I know your [record of] works and what you are doing; you are neither cold nor hot. Would that you were cold or hot!
16
So, because you are lukewarm and neither cold nor hot, I will spew you out of My mouth!

17
For you say, I am rich; I have prospered and grown wealthy, and I am in need of nothing; and you do not realize and understand that you are wretched, pitiable, poor, blind, and naked.
18
*Therefore I counsel you to **purchase from Me gold refined and tested by fire**, that you may be [truly] wealthy, and white clothes to clothe you and to keep the shame of your nudity from being seen, and salve to put on your eyes, that you may see.*

To neither be cold nor hot means to be neither completely dead nor full of zeal, but indifferent and careless. This is the last church that John writes about in Revelation. To me this passage hits home in the churches of America. God asks us to buy pure gold! He is asking us to do righteous exchanges again; to do business on God's terms and not on our own. I have been in prayer for revival, where our zeal is not oppressing those who make "bad" choices, but our zeal is in His love for all people!

CHAPTER FIVE

WHO DOES THE EARTH
BELONG TO?

> ## *Philippians 2:5-8 (NKJV)*
> **5**
> *Let this mind be in you which was also in Christ Jesus,*
> **6**
> *who, being in the form of God, did not consider it robbery to be equal with God,*
> **7**
> *but made Himself of no reputation, taking the form of a bondservant, and coming in the likeness of men.*
> **8**
> *And being found in appearance as a man, He humbled Himself and became obedient to the point of death, even the death of the cross.*

We have seen that Christ humbled Himself from the divine form to human form, and from incorruptible to corruptible FLESH.

The Holy Spirit spoke into my heart one day and said, "The physical IS spiritual." That phrase really messed up my Christian thinking! To me it seemed like the only time physical things mattered in the church was when someone physically sinned, but as far as the beauty and mystery of the physical, that was overlooked or looked down upon. I noticed in the Word of God that the separation between the physical and spiritual is usually between mammon and the true gold, or Satan's seen kingdom and God's unseen Kingdom. In other words the Bible never tells us to ignore the physical. As a matter of fact our entire salvation is based off of the physical flesh of a man!

> ### *Acts 2:29-32 (NKJV)*
> **29**
> *"Men and brethren, let me speak freely to you of the patriarch David, that he is both dead and buried, and his tomb is with us to this day.*
> **30**
> *Therefore, being a prophet, and knowing that God had sworn with an oath to him that of the fruit of his body, according to the flesh, He would raise up the Christ to sit on his throne,*
> **31**
> *he, foreseeing this, spoke concerning the resurrection of the Christ, that His soul was not left in Hades, nor did His flesh see corruption.*
> **32**
> *This Jesus God has raised up, of which we are all witnesses.*

This passage is when Peter is preaching after the one hundred and twenty in the upper room all get filled with the Holy Ghost and fire! Peter said that the flesh of the Lord did not see corruption! His physical flesh did not rot in the ground, but the Father raised Him from the dead after three days with an incorruptible flesh! The flesh of Jesus went from corruptible to incorruptible!

1 Corinthians 15:42-44 (NKJV)

42

So also is the resurrection of the dead. The body is sown in corruption, it is raised in incorruption.

43

It is sown in dishonor, it is raised in glory. It is sown in weakness, it is raised in power.

44

It is sown a natural body, it is raised a spiritual body. There is a natural body, and there is a spiritual body.

The natural body will become a spiritual body! This means that the body will become immortal in its substance. The Bible shows no reference of our bodies becoming immaterial, intangible, and without flesh and bone. Our flesh, just like the flesh of Jesus, will go from corruptible (because of sin) to incorruptible (because of Grace)! "Our bodies will still be our bodies."

- Finis Dake

Genesis 2:7 (NKJV)

And the Lord God formed man of the dust of the ground, and breathed into his nostrils the breath of life; and man became a living being.

The body was formed out of the earth, but the soul and the spirit were created.

Genesis 3:19 (NKJV)

In the sweat of your face you shall eat bread Till you return to the ground, For out of it you were taken; For dust you are, And to dust you shall return. "

From dust/earth I am, and to the dust/earth I shall return. One-third of each of us has been formed out of an already created body! Jesus has the same type of body formed out of the earth, but it has already been made incorruptible for eternity! We're getting somewhere!

Romans 8:18-23 (NKJV)

18

For I consider that the sufferings of this present time are not worthy to be compared with the glory which shall be revealed in us.

19

For the earnest expectation of the creation eagerly waits for the revealing of the sons of God.

20

For the creation was subjected to futility, not willingly, but because of Him who subjected it in hope;

21

because the creation itself also will be delivered from the bondage of corruption into the glorious liberty of the children of God.

22

For we know that the whole creation groans and labors with birth pangs together until now.

23

*Not only that, but we also who have the
firstfruits of the Spirit, even we ourselves
groan within ourselves, eagerly waiting for
the adoption, the redemption of our body.*

Creation is eager to see us revealed! Why? Number one: because creation was also subjected to the curse. However creation itself, earth itself, will not be stuck under the curse forever! The earth will not remain under the curse because of mankind, because of you and me! What birth pangs does the earth have? We know that part of the curse was that women would have pain during child birth. We, the Church, are the Bride (woman) of Christ (flesh/God).

We are made out of dust, out of this earth. We were birthed out of this creation/earth in pain, due to the curse!

Number two; because we were children of this earth, and through us, who become the children of God; WE lead the body of the earth from corruption to incorruption!

Mankind, made from the dirt, becomes like God. Part of the earth becomes like God!! That is why the earth cannot wait! I groan for the redemption of my body, and the earth groans for the redemption of her body!

As the Holy Spirit began to unravel these facts before me, I was blown away! I began to see that I should enjoy this earth; all the trees, oceans, seas, landscapes, animals, and plants. Most of my learned Christianity had taken that away from me, almost condemning me for being too "New Age"; when in fact, this is a pivotal part of being one with the Creator. In 1 Corinthians 15:39-42 we are taught that there are different types of bodies of creation. One of those bodies is the earth, and the human body was formed from it.

2 Corinthians 4:7 (NKJV)
But we have this treasure in earthen vessels, that the excellence of the power may be of God and not of us.

Mankind, here called an earthen vessel, carries a treasure inside that will turn the dirt it is formed of from corruption to incorruption! Since part of the earth is in all of mankind, the earth is longing for those who believe, the sons and daughters of God, to change into that everlasting spiritual body so she can, too.

According to Romans 1:20 creation is the one thing that prevents mankind from having an excuse for not believing in God. Wow! Creation itself displays the visible attributes of the invisible God! In Colossians 1:15 it says that Jesus is the image of the invisible God! Jesus who was and is made from this body we call the earth.

One reason many believers don't know about this is because they have been taught that this old earth is going to be burned up with fire anyway. Anyone ever been taught that? Here is where they get that teaching:

2 Peter 3:10-11 (NKJV)
10
But the day of the Lord will come as a thief in the night, in which the heavens will pass away with a great noise, and the elements will melt with fervent heat; both the earth and the works that are in it will be burned up.

11
Therefore, since all these things will be dissolved, what manner of persons ought you to be in holy conduct and godliness,

The word "heavens" in this passage is not where the throne of God is; it means the earth's atmosphere. The Bible translates this word many times as "heavenlies." We have already learned that it is in the heavenlies where the principalities, powers, and demonic strongholds are situated.

The two words "pass away" mean to pass from one condition to another. Those words never mean annihilation.

The word "elements" refers to "the principles or basic elements of the present world's system of evil spirits, sinful and fallen nature, disease, germs, corruptions, and all elements by which men corrupt themselves."

- Finis Dake

The phrase "fervent heat" is the same heat that burns away all of our impurities until we become pure gold.

What Peter is saying is that on this Day of the Lord the earth and all of creation will become new, not a new physical earth, but it will pass from corruption into incorruption! Revelation 21 speaks of this day too. This is about the day that the Sons of God are revealed!

1 Corinthians 15:25-26 (NKJV)
25
For He must reign till He has put all enemies under His feet.

THE ETERNAL PURPOSE OF MANKIND

> *26*
> *The last enemy that will be destroyed is death.*

Sin was the only thing that made this physical world and these bodies corruptible, but DEATH will be put under; not the creation.

> ### Matthew 6:10 (NKJV)
> *Your kingdom come. Your will be done. On Earth as it is in heaven.*

I have written all of that to show you that the EARTH is our domain. This is why I can legally pray His Kingdom HERE TO EARTH! Heaven is not my final destination, this earth is my home. I came from earth, but I have been re-born of God. We are the rulers of this planet; it belongs to us!

> ### Proverbs 10:30 (NKJV)
> *The righteous will never be removed, But the wicked will not inhabit the earth.*

> ### Matthew 5:5 (NKJV)
> *Blessed are the meek, or they shall inherit the earth.*

The earth will belong to you and me for eternity; God does not create things to destroy them. This earth used to belong to Lucifer, a created angel. Yet God took part of this very planet, formed a being from it, and put a soul and spirit inside of it to rule and reign as part of the earth and as part of God!

SECTION TWO

IDENTITY

CHAPTER SIX

THE EXCHANGE TABLE

On November 14, 2013 I had a vision of Jesus. Our small church was singing to heaven and worshipping God, but nobody knew that I was struggling that night. I had so many cares and worries, heavy weights upon my shoulders. Money was low, there were issues with members of the congregation, and I was battling something physical in my body. As the chorus of people rang around me, I closed my eyes and imagined myself pushing all of those weights over to Jesus. I remember trying to hide my tears from the congregation because I needed God's help; I needed rest in my mind.

As I continued to push through, with my eyes still closed, a scene played before me like a dream. I saw a large rectangular wooden table. I began to look up and saw Jesus sitting behind the table. It was Him. He sat there and looked at me as if this was His profession. I cried out to Him, and over this long wooden table I pushed all of my cares, worries, and weights to Him. He took them, and in exchange He pushed back a replacement for each thing I had given over to Him. I felt relieved and light. He looked at me, smiled, and said, "You should do the exchange more often." Immediately I was conscious again of the church building and the people around me as they continued to worship and lift up the Name of Jesus.

2 Corinthians 5:21 (NKJV)
For He made Him who knew no sin to be

sin for us, that we might become the righteousness of God in Him.

Jesus became sin. In other words Jesus took our sin and gave us His righteousness! We can say that we exchanged our sin at His table for His righteousness!! Many believers call this the Great Exchange or the Beautiful Exchange. I knew this well, and I knew that there was an exchange at our redemption!

Isaiah 53:4-5 (AMPC)
4
*Surely He has **borne** our griefs (sicknesses, weaknesses, and distresses) and carried our sorrows and pains [of punishment], yet we [ignorantly] considered Him stricken, smitten, and afflicted by God [as if with leprosy].*
5
But He was wounded for our transgressions, He was bruised for our guilt and iniquities; the chastisement [needful to obtain] peace and well-being for us was upon Him, and with the stripes [that wounded] Him we are healed and made whole.

The Holy Spirit began to show me that there were many exchanges at the cross. The word "borne" in Isaiah is the idea of one person taking the burden of another and placing it upon themselves. Here is another exchange: we can exchange our poverty for His riches!

2 Corinthians 8:9 (NKJV)
For you know the grace of our Lord Jesus

Christ, that though He was rich, yet for your sakes He became poor, that you through His poverty might become rich.

The easiest way to put it is this: **we can exchange what we lack for what He provides!**

A few days after having the vision of Jesus, I began to ask the Holy Spirit to reveal more to me, I wanted Him to open my eyes to the fullness of what He had shown me. One day I heard Him speak to me! He said, "The sanctuaries of worship were always meant for exchange and trade. He sits in the House of God at the table of God's fair and just exchanges, to make all the exchanges provided at the cross. Lucifer used to exchange pure gold in the sanctuaries of God, that's why Jesus overthrew the tables."

Wow! That was a lot to sink in! Whenever I receive a revelation from God I do my best to make sure it is backed by His Word. Remember in Ezekiel 28:18 it says, "you have defiled your sanctuaries by unrighteous trade"? The word "sanctuary" is the same as the House of Worship. In Romans 14:17 it says the **Kingdom of God is righteousness**, peace, and joy in the Holy Spirit! God's Kingdom is righteous. The devil's kingdom is unrighteous, unfair, and unjust. Lucifer was making a trade or exchange outside of God's parameters, outside of God's Kingdom. Lucifer created his own kingdom separate from God! He went from trading pure gold to trading impure gold.

Revelation 3:15-22 (NKJV)
15
"I know your works, that you are neither cold nor hot. I could wish you were cold or hot.

16

So then, because you are lukewarm, and neither cold nor hot,[a] I will vomit you out of My mouth.

17

Because you say, 'I am rich, have become wealthy, and have need of nothing'—and do not know that you are wretched, miserable, poor, blind, and naked—

18

I counsel you to buy from Me gold refined in the fire, that you may be rich; *and white garments, that you may be clothed, that the shame of your nakedness may not be revealed; and anoint your eyes with eye salve, that you may see.*

19

As many as I love, I rebuke and chasten. Therefore be zealous and repent.

20

Behold, I stand at the door and knock. If anyone hears My voice and opens the door, I will come in to him and dine with him, and he with Me.

21

To him who overcomes I will grant to sit with Me on My throne, as I also overcame and sat down with My Father on His throne.

22

"He who has an ear, let him hear what the Spirit says to the churches." ' "

There are two kinds of gold, pure and impure. We have already learned that pure gold is our faith. We "buy" with faith! That's awesome!

As mentioned before (in Matthew 21:12-17) when Jesus overturns the tables in the temple, He drove out the unfair exchanges, and instead brought righteous exchanges back into the house of worship! He overthrew the **tables** that Satan had created and put the correct **tables** of exchange back in the house of God! Jesus is sitting behind that exchange table because it really is His business!

> ### *Isaiah 55:1-2 (AMPC)*
> *1*
> *Wait and listen, everyone who is thirsty! Come to the waters; and **he who has no money, come, buy and eat! Yes, come, buy [priceless, spiritual] wine and milk without money and without price [simply for the self-surrender that accepts the blessing].***
> *2*
> *Why do you spend your money for that which is not bread, and your earnings for what does not satisfy? Hearken diligently to Me, and eat what is good, and let your soul delight itself in fatness [the profuseness of spiritual joy].*

The Bible is telling us to come, buy and eat, *but not to purchase with money.* To purchase without a price! You and I can come and quench our thirst by exchange at God's table; we don't have to have money or impure gold to do so. What do we purchase with here? Self-surrender! All of MY junk, cares, worry, anxiety, sickness, depression and weight; I surrender what is mine for what is His!

Hebrews 4:14-16 (NKJV)

14
Seeing then that we have a great High Priest who has passed through the heavens, Jesus the Son of God, let us hold fast our confession.

15
For we do not have a High Priest who cannot sympathize with our weaknesses, but was in all points tempted as we are, yet without sin.

16
Let us therefore come boldly to the throne of grace, that we may obtain mercy and find grace to help in time of need.

Hold fast to our confession of what? It's the confession of our weaknesses and temptations! We are to come to Him boldly. Boldly means with "all outspokenness"! **We are to come into the throne room of Grace with all outspokenness about our weaknesses and temptations!** We give Jesus the real us in exchange for the real Him! This is the opposite of what I've seen happen in many churches. People tend to lie about their faults, failures, and temptations, and I do not blame them one bit! The Body of Christ has allowed more mercy and grace for themselves than for any others. I believe because the Church has been condemning - we have taught people to be scared; not only to come and tell their brothers and sisters in Christ their faults, but to be frightened out of their minds to even tell God the TRUTH!

The reason Jesus had to tell me to do the exchange more often is because no one ever told me that Jesus is waiting to take my JUNK! We have been taught to get rid of our junk first *so we can be able to go* to Jesus. We have had it backwards! **Jesus loves to take your sin, anger, bitterness, questions, hurts, disappointments, and heaviness. He cannot wait to take it so that He can give you righteousness, peace, forgiveness, answers, wholeness, hope, and life abundantly! This is the table of exchange.** (Luke 22:29-30; Matthew 15:22-28)

Psalm 23:1-6 (NKJV)
1
The Lord is my shepherd; I shall not want.
2
He makes me to lie down in green pastures; He leads me beside the still waters.
3
He restores my soul; He leads me in the paths of righteousness For His name's sake.
4
Yea, though I walk through the valley of the shadow of death, I will fear no evil; For You are with me; Your rod and Your staff, they comfort me.
5
You prepare a table before me in the presence of my enemies; You anoint my head with oil; My cup runs over.
6
Surely goodness and mercy shall follow me All the days of my life; And I will dwell in the house of the Lord Forever.

Even when you are in the valley, even when your enemies surround you, a table is put in your midst so that you can continue to make exchanges with your God! You can cry out to God in the middle of all hell breaking loose in your life. You can come boldly when you have made a mistake! **You and I worship God by giving Him our sin and our junk!** We exchange it and freely receive back everything that He suffered and died for. That was the point of His suffering!

I challenge you in this very moment while reading this book to STOP. Are you ready to worship God for one minute? Are you ready to spill your heart, thoughts, and emotions to the Father? Does it feel weird to tell God things on your heart in the same way you would tell your best friend? It felt weird for me at first. I yelled and cried, shouted and screamed until I got it all out in God's throne room. God didn't get mad at me. He loved me, and He gave me everything I needed. This chapter is the foundation to understanding who we truly are - our identity.

GOD'S GLORY

2 Corinthians 3:16-18 (NKJV)

16

Nevertheless when one turns to the Lord, the veil is taken away.

17

Now the Lord is the Spirit; and where the Spirit of the Lord is, there is liberty.

18

But we all, with unveiled face, beholding as in a mirror the glory of the Lord, are being transformed into the same image from glory to glory, *just as by the Spirit of the Lord.*

2 Corinthians 4:1-7 (NKJV)

1

Therefore, since we have this ministry, *as we have received mercy, we do not lose heart.*

2

But we have renounced the hidden things of shame, not walking in craftiness nor handling the word of God deceitfully, but by manifestation of the truth commending ourselves to every man's conscience in the sight of God.

3

But even if our gospel is veiled, it is veiled to those who are perishing,

4

whose minds the god of this age has blinded, who do not believe, lest the light of the gospel of the glory of Christ, who is the image of God, should shine on them.

5

For we do not preach ourselves, but Christ Jesus the Lord, and ourselves your bondservants for Jesus' sake.

6

For it is the God who commanded light to shine out of darkness, who has shone in our hearts to give the light of the knowledge of the glory of God in the face of Jesus Christ.

7

But we have this treasure in earthen vessels, that the excellence of the power may be of God and not of us.

The Bible says we are beholding the GLORY of God as in a mirror. Who do we see in a mirror? The Word says that we are transformed into the SAME IMAGE of Jesus, from Glory to Glory, by the Holy Spirit! It goes on to say, "THEREFORE since we have this MINISTRY." What ministry? In this context it's the ministry of Jesus! The ministry of Jesus was and is the ministry of the Glory of God. Jesus was and is the GLORY of God by the power of the Holy Spirit! **Our ministry is to become the GLORY of God by that same power!**

Romans 8:30 (NKJV)
Moreover whom He predestined, these He also called; whom He called, these He also justified; and whom He justified, these He also glorified.

The end result to all destiny, calling, and righteousness is to be glorified! We will one day possess glorified immortal bodies. This is not a one-time transformation at the end of all days; this is a continual manifestation by the Holy Spirit as we go from glory to glory. Jesus was and is the Father's glory, but now you and I have taken His place on this earth. **We are the glory of the Father!**

The definition of glory is the highest praise and honor; the source of honor, fame, and admiration; thanksgiving. If we are the glory of God then we are God's highest praise and honor! We are God's source of honor, fame, and admiration! God is thankful for the human race that He created. We are taking the place of Lucifer on this planet and bringing God His due glory.

In 2 Corinthians 4:6, we see that God commanded light to shine out of darkness. This light has shone or it has lit up our hearts and spirits. For what purpose? For the purpose to GIVE the light of the knowledge of the GLORY of God by personal relationship with Jesus, the GLORY of God. God commanded light into our hearts so that we could see what is in our hearts. God desperately wants us to see that God's GLORY is within us; it's the treasure inside this earthen vessel! **God commanded light to shine in our hearts for the purpose that this light (Jesus) would give us the knowledge that we are the very GLORY of God!**

I hear people sing worship songs to God. They say, "I give you all the glory." That should have more meaning to us now. We're telling God that we give Him all of us! His glory is the treasure within us. The context of what Paul referenced as hidden treasures within us is awesome.

> **"Treasures were hidden in earthen vessels to protect them from the damp. Here it refers to the power of the Holy Spirit through the light of Jesus in our physical bodies. The emphasis is on the contrast between a frail vessel of earth and the priceless treasure of power that dwells in us!"**
>
> **- Finis Dake**

The **Glory** of an immortal God is already placed inside of mortal human bodies, and the **Glory** will transform our mortal bodies into immortal bodies very soon!

2 Corinthians 4:7-10 (NKJV)

7

But we have this treasure in earthen vessels, that the excellence of the power may be of God and not of us.

8

We are hard-pressed on every side, yet not crushed; we are perplexed, but not in despair;

9

persecuted, but not forsaken; struck down, but not destroyed—

10

always carrying about in the body the dying of the Lord Jesus, that the life of Jesus also may be manifested in our body.

We are always carrying in our bodies the dying of Jesus, the glory of God. We are allowing death to ourselves so that the life, the glory of Jesus, would manifest in our actual, physical bodies! **The glory of God manifests in our physical bodies when we EXCHANGE our sin for His GLORY!**

> *2 Corinthians 4:16-18 (NKJV)*
> *16*
> *Therefore we do not lose heart. Even though our outward man is perishing, yet the inward man is being renewed day by day.*
> *17*
> ***For our light affliction, which is but for a moment, is working for us a far more exceeding and eternal weight of glory,***
> *18*
> *while we do not look at the things which are seen, but at the things which are not seen. For the things which are seen are temporary, but the things which are not seen are eternal.*

Our light affliction is for a very short amount of time! **The best part is not that it is very short. The best part is that the affliction is doing the work for us!** What work is affliction doing for us? The work to mold us into eternal glory, a weight of glory that far exceeds the pain and suffering of this present time!

Jonathan Edwards said, "The weight of glory is the weight of all that God is, the fullness of His understanding, virtue, and happiness."

That means that you and I are the fullness of God's understanding, virtue, and happiness! Are you beginning to see who you really are yet? You are not simply just loved by God. You have a destiny with Him, full of purpose, honor, and glory that all belongs to Him!

> ### *Romans 8:16-19 (NKJV)*
> *16*
> *The Spirit Himself bears witness with our spirit that we are children of God,*
> *17*
> *and if children, then heirs—heirs of God and joint heirs with Christ, **if indeed we suffer with Him, that we may also be glorified together.***
> *18*
> ***For I consider that the sufferings of this present time are not worthy to be compared with the glory which shall be revealed in us.***
> *19*
> *For the earnest expectation of the creation eagerly waits for the revealing of the sons of God.*

If we suffer with Jesus, or for His Name's sake, we will be glorified with Jesus. Again Paul states that this suffering for Jesus cannot be compared to the glory to be revealed IN US! I want you to catch this. Where is the glory of God revealed? **IN US!** All of creation is waiting for you and me, the glory of God, to be revealed!

The Holy Spirit has spoken to me, as well as many other children of God, saying that His GLORY will cover entire cities! Habakkuk 2:14 states that "the earth will be filled

With the knowledge of the glory of the Lord, As the waters cover the sea." We are His glory! The glory of God is within these earthen vessels! The more people understand who they really are, the more the glory of God manifests to cover this entire earth!

We say, "Show me Your glory." The more we give ourselves to Him the more glory we will see. If we want His glory to fall, we must give Him all of us, because we are the glory. We lose our life to find it. We give Him the glory. This is why we need to understand the exchange table. The greatness of the exchange is my life for His glory! We become the pure gold of exchange. God, who is pure gold, exchanged His life for us, in our impure state. We are becoming the pure gold, just like God, as His glory for eternity.

First Corinthians 11:7 says that the wife is the glory of her husband. In numerous places we are called the Bride of Christ. We are the glory of our husband. We are the glory of God. His glory will fill this earth! His glory will fill the universe!

CHAPTER EIGHT

GOD'S WORSHIP

Music is a powerful gift given to mankind from God. Some people say that they have had spiritual experiences while listening to or playing music under the influence of a substance. Intoxication by drugs and alcohol is a cheap counterfeit to the presence of the Spirit of God. Music, like drugs, is always connected to a spirit. This type of spirit moves us and can change our thoughts and intentions of the heart. An artist may yield to a spirit to create music. If you are a music lover like I am, then you will understand that rhythm is key. The Holy Spirit moves in a rhythm too. Music is a physical reaction to a spiritual (heart) move. Music puts rhythm to the spirit. This is true even before lyrics are added to the music. Lyrics simply make heart motives more clear. We are able to feel the power in music, and sometimes it's not from the anointing, but from a demonic counterfeit of the Holy Spirit.

2 Kings 3:14-16 (NKJV)
14
And Elisha said, "As the Lord of hosts lives, before whom I stand, surely were it not that I regard the presence of Jehoshaphat king of Judah, I would not look at you, nor see you.
15
But now bring me a musician." ***Then it***

happened, when the musician played,
that the hand of the Lord came upon him.
16
***And he said**, "Thus says the Lord: 'Make*
this valley full of ditches.'

I love this passage. Elisha prophesied under the anointing as the music was being played, without words!

1 Chronicles 25:1 (NKJV)
Moreover David and the captains of the army separated for the service some of the sons of Asaph, of Heman, and of Jeduthun, **who should prophesy with harps, stringed instruments, and cymbals.** *And the number of the skilled men performing their service was:*

1 Chronicles 25:6 (NKJV)
All these were under the direction of their father for the music in the house of the Lord, with cymbals, stringed instruments, and harps, for the service of the house of God. Asaph, Jeduthun, and Heman were under the authority of the king.

In this story they had 288 skilled musicians and singers for the house of the Lord. Again, the musicians prophesied with the music itself, without words. Music is an anointed partner to the gifts of the Holy Spirit.

1 Samuel 16:13-23 (NKJV)
13
Then Samuel took the horn of oil and anointed him in the midst of his brothers;

and the Spirit of the Lord came upon David from that day forward. So Samuel arose and went to Ramah. A Distressing Spirit Troubles Saul

14

But the Spirit of the Lord departed from Saul, and a distressing spirit from the Lord troubled him.

15

And Saul's servants said to him, "Surely, a distressing spirit from God is troubling you.

16

Let our master now command your servants, who are before you, to seek out a man who is a skillful player on the harp. And it shall be that he will play it with his hand when the distressing spirit from God is upon you, and you shall be well."

17

So Saul said to his servants, "Provide me now a man who can play well, and bring him to me."

18

Then one of the servants answered and said, "Look, I have seen a son of Jesse the Bethlehemite, who is skillful in playing, a mighty man of valor, a man of war, prudent in speech, and a handsome person; and the Lord is with him."

19

Therefore Saul sent messengers to Jesse, and said, "Send me your son David, who is with the sheep."

20

And Jesse took a donkey loaded with bread,

*a skin of wine, and a young goat, and sent
them by his son David to Saul.*

21

*So David came to Saul and stood before
him. And he loved him greatly, and he
became his armorbearer.*

22

*Then Saul sent to Jesse, saying, "Please
let David stand before me, for he has found
favor in my sight."*

23

*And so it was, whenever the spirit from
God was upon Saul, that David would take
a harp and play it with his hand. Then Saul
would become refreshed and well, and the
distressing spirit would depart from him.*

The Bible says that the Holy Spirit came upon David, but
left Saul. Notice that the word "spirit" here is not capitalized.
A better rendering for this passage is that God allowed a
distressing spirit to come upon Saul. Why? Saul no longer
had the Holy Spirit. God gave Saul over to an evil spirit,
which had an open door to come in since the Spirit of the
living God had left him. We see music without words, anointed
by the Holy Spirit, casting evil spirits away from a king who
no longer had the Spirit of God. This is amazing. (1 Corinthians
14:15; Ephesians 5:15-21)

Since music itself has a spirit, to listen to music with lyrics
about things like sex, drugs, anger, depression, or anything
other than Christ seems to be unprofitable. **However, even
more than this we should seek to *create* anointed music
that destroys the works of the devil!** Songs from heaven
that break the chains of the enemy, like David's did!

Isaiah 14:11-13 (NKJV)

11

*Your pomp is brought down to Sheol, **And the sound of your stringed instruments;** The maggot is spread under you, And worms cover you.' The Fall of Lucifer*

12

"How you are fallen from heaven, O Lucifer,[a] son of the morning! How you are cut down to the ground, You who weakened the nations!

13

For you have said in your heart: 'I will ascend into heaven, I will exalt my throne above the stars of God; I will also sit on the mount of the congregation On the farthest sides of the north;

Lucifer was the morning star. This passage tells us he had stringed instruments.

Ezekiel 28:13 (NKJV)

*You were in Eden, the garden of God; Every precious stone was your covering: The sardius, topaz, and diamond, Beryl, onyx, and jasper, Sapphire, turquoise, and emerald with gold. **The workmanship of your timbrels and pipes Was prepared for you on the day you were created.***

Timbrels are a drumhead. Pipes refer to a wind instrument.

Job 38:7 (NKJV)

When the morning stars sang together, And all the sons of God shouted for joy?

The morning stars sang together, and Lucifer was called the morning star. Remember how Lucifer was called the "anointed cherub"? According to Ezekiel, a cherubim's purpose is to worship God, especially with music!

Lucifer was trading pure gold through intimate worship in the sanctuaries of worship at one time. However, by unrighteous trade and exchange, Satan created a counterfeit worship and music. We can bring the glory back into the House of Worship again by exchanging our junk for the pure gold because of Jesus! In other words, **in this exchange we do not just receive SOMETHING back, we receive SOMEONE back. Who do we receive back? It's us, our true identity! We become the exchanged substance, the gold and the glory of God, the very thing that Lucifer himself coveted after he made unrighteous exchanges. We literally become the *worship* of God by becoming His glory. Lucifer exchanged the true glory and worship *for a substance he could possess*; however, we make exchanges to literally *become the substance*!** Re-read this paragraph a few times. Read it until it hits your spirit and it comes alive.

Lucifer was involved in intimate worship and exchange. **Since the fall of Lucifer, the human race has REPLACED him and his angels as instruments of worship!** God inhabits the praises of His people! (Psalm 22:3) **God inhabits our praises because ON EARTH we are the worship of HEAVEN!** We are God's Kingdom on this earth by remaining in constant exchange as new creations that have been transformed from glory to glory as the essence of all that He is, **as worship unto Himself!** God worships Himself through you, through me, through our existence!

I am God's worship. The highest form of worship is not exchanging at the table, but becoming the worship. We become the gold. To see the gold we must allow trials to burn away the rubble. **When I stand and trust God and count it all joy in every circumstance and trial, I BECOME the very essence of worship!** When I live in sin I can only worship by my actions and works. However, when I live a holy life and allow the trial to burn away the sin in joy, I *become* the worship. I thank God for His Grace. When we allow the fire of the trial to burn us down to untainted gold, we become what God **WANTS**. **I am the pure gold a jealous God WANTS to be RICH off of in His own Kingdom** because I am His very worship. I am His glory!

Matthew 13:44 (NKJV)
"Again, the kingdom of heaven is like treasure hidden in a field, which a man found and hid; and for joy over it he goes and sells all that he has and buys that field.

God is rich because He possesses *us*. We are His gold. God bought us with the precious Blood of Jesus Christ. We are the ones in the field. We are the treasure! The exchange was that He was rich and became poor so I could be rich, but He became poor and is now rich by purchasing us with His Blood! He is jealous for you. God becomes everything to us, and we become everything to Him.

CHAPTER NINE

THE WOODEN CROSS

The vision of the exchange table had changed my life. As I was seeking the Lord regarding what I had seen, the Holy Spirit asked me this question: ''Why was the exchange table in the vision made out of wood?'' I knew immediately. The exchange table is the cross!

Galatians 3:10-14 (NKJV)
10
For as many as are of the works of the law are under the curse; for it is written, "Cursed is everyone who does not continue in all things which are written in the book of the law, to do them."
11
But that no one is justified by the law in the sight of God is evident, for "the just shall live by faith."
12
Yet the law is not of faith, but "the man who does them shall live by them."
13
Christ has redeemed us from the curse of the law, having become a curse for us (for it is written, "Cursed is everyone who hangs on a tree"),

14

that the blessing of Abraham might come upon the Gentiles in Christ Jesus, that we might receive the promise of the Spirit through faith.

To sum this up, a tree that once represented the curse now represents the blessing by the exchange! Not only do we exchange at the wooden table, but we actually become the exchanged **substance** upon the table, the gold of God. When we get up on that table and become the exchanged worship and gold, we lay down upon the cross!

<u>Matthew 16:24-27 (NKJV)</u>
24

Then Jesus said to His disciples, "If anyone desires to come after Me, let him deny himself, and take up his cross, and follow Me.
25

For whoever desires to save his life will lose it, but whoever loses his life for My sake will find it.
26

For what profit is it to a man if he gains the whole world, and loses his own soul? Or what will a man give in exchange for his soul?
27

For the Son of Man will come in the glory of His Father with His angels, and then He will reward each according to his works.

What does it mean to take up your cross and follow Jesus? It means to deny yourself to the extent of all that you are becoming - the gold upon the wooden table. There is an exchange made on man's side for man to see God's side. Jesus asked, "What profit/gain do you make exchanging your LIFE for Satan's kingdom?" People will give up who they have become to gain ground in one kingdom or the other. However, the greatest gain is in exchanging your life for God's Kingdom!

What is our cross? The exchange table is our cross! **Our cross is His cross as the blessing and not the curse!** The blessing is His Grace that gives us the ability to lay down our LIFE upon that cross. This is why the highest form of worship is on the table; it's giving Jesus our LIFE! **We are exchanging our life for HIS LIFE, and life more abundantly.**

On the cross (at the exchange table) is the only place where you and I become like God. Jesus became glorified after getting on the cross. Jesus is our example of what we can and should do. When we give all of our life to Him we become just like Him, and this is precisely how He gets His worship. This is how His cup runs over. The cross is not a heavy burden of sickness, disease, poverty, and oppression. It is a true sacrifice for us because we exchange everything that we are for His all! The cross still hurts us, just not in the way of sickness and poverty. **All the emotional things we hold onto as our identity die upon that cross so that we can become like Him, and not like us!** I don't know about you, but I would rather be like God than myself!

To get on the exchange table means that our heart and spirit are changing into God's. It's giving God our mind, will, and emotions so that He can give us His. When we say things such as, "I'm like such and such," and define ourselves by things that are created and pass away, it defies the process of becoming like Christ. **How can I keep my own identity and take on His identity?** This can be very difficult for people. We identify with styles, clothes, music, culture, entertainment, skills, gifts, status, money, personality....on and on we could go. The Word of God, the Bible, tells us who we really are meant to be. Our feelings, education, and experiences have nothing to do *with WHO we really are.* The world asks, "What do you do?" The Body of Christ should ask, "Who are you?" This is our suffering, this is our cross to carry, to become like the Living God; to actually find our life by losing it. We are all unique and beautiful expressions of His multifaceted wisdom. We can actually never be unique and set apart outside of Him; anything outside of Him is common to the rest of creation. I believe this is the missing link. **Those who want to be like God but will never stop being themselves.** Who are you? Why did God make you? Are you beginning to see that you were created to be like God? We have to lose this false identity that Satan has deceived us into thinking we are. I'm created to be like God!

One day the Lord spoke to me regarding these things. He said, "Stop pretending you want to be like Me. The exchange to having the money you want, the health, etc. is a larger exchange than you're acting like it is. You haven't received all of My exchanged favor and blessing because I haven't received your pride, personality, and spouse." That shook me up! I realized we all hold on to things like a back-up if God is not as good as we say He is. The Holy Spirit was waking me up and showing me that I actually had a lack of trust in Him.

Remember in Isaiah 55:1-2 the Bible tells us to come and buy without money? **Our heart/our spirit is the treasure and the gold, the only thing that can be exchanged for**

eternal glory. When I give God my heart He gives me His Spirit! When we crawl onto that cross, our spirits become ruler over our souls (mind, will, and emotions) and flesh (body). No longer do our feelings dictate our reality. No longer do our painful experiences tell us what we can and cannot accomplish. Now our spirits, our hearts, have become like God! **Now we can be just like God!** We put our souls and bodies upon the wooden cross; they die so that our spirits can rule like His.

To be like God, I give all three parts of me (spirit, soul, and body) to Him. He takes my spirit and makes it just like His! Once my spirit is like God's, I have the ability to put my own flesh and soul onto the cross as my worship according to what just happened in my spirit! No one can crucify the flesh if his or her heart hasn't been given to God. It was Jesus who defeated sin! Our spirits have to become like all powerful God before we can say no to the flesh and rule our entire being. How do I starve the appetite of the flesh and soul? By recognizing I have the grace to be just like God!

The Lord continued to speak to me, "Be like Me. You do not know what you are capable of. Many come to the cross (exchange table), but few take up their cross (get onto the table/become the exchanged substance). The cross draws them, but they are afraid to become like Me. They do not see that the cross is the power to be like God! It is a tree of Life; it killed My first Son and gives life to all who come, buy, and exchange."

2 Corinthians 9:6-11 (NKJV)
6
But this I say: He who sows sparingly will also reap sparingly, and he who sows bountifully will also reap bountifully.

7

So let each one give as he purposes in his heart, not grudgingly or of necessity; for God loves a cheerful giver.

8

And God is able to make all grace abound toward you, that you, always having all sufficiency in all things, may have an abundance for every good work.

9

As it is written: "He has dispersed abroad, He has given to the poor; His righteousness endures forever."

10

Now may He who supplies seed to the sower, and bread for food, supply and multiply the seed you have sown and increase the fruits of your righteousness,

11

while you are enriched in everything for all liberality, which causes thanksgiving through us to God.

Sowing seed is a form of exchange. We exchange a seed for a tree that will produce fruit. However, so many times we use our seed thinking it's the fruit of a grown tree. This is usually because patience has not had its perfect work in us yet. Be careful not to spend your seed! A seed represents planting and death. The seed is planted, and then dies, so the tree can begin to grow. Did you know that you are a seed? We have to die for the tree to grow. Do I need to tell you to let the cross grow? Let yourself die upon that cross so that a tree of blessing can come forth and make you like God! **We lay down on that cross and it stands up (grows) like a**

tree and WE BECOME THE FRUIT! Awesome! You and I are the fruit of the cross!

We need to find out what our seed actually is, don't' we? The seed can be anything we hold onto as our identity. It could be our money, our talents, our gifts, our time, our personalities. Sowing the seed is death to those things in our lives that have identified us over our identity in Christ. We exchange our money for His money, our talents for His talents, our gifts for the Gifts of the Holy Spirit, our timing for His timing, His personality, His character and on and on we exchange! We take these things to Him and say, "God, I give these things to you for Your glory, and not for mine anymore."

God had to tell me to stop glorifying the seed I received at the exchange table and sow it (bury it) so I could become like Jesus from the inside out! I challenge you to let all of "you" die and become God's very personality of joy, peace, and righteousness. In this way He is glorified in us; Jesus shows and all people are drawn to Him. God is drawing more wealth unto Himself!

HEART

CHAPTER TEN

BACK TO MY FIRST LOVE

To humiliate the devil and to become like God; this is our eternal purpose. This is who we really are. As more and more was being revealed to me about our purpose in humiliating the devil and becoming just like God, I began to desire that deeper relationship with Him. Relationship without purpose is meaningless and empty. However, purpose without relationship will begin to be too difficult and life becomes desperately lonely. I remember when I taught these revelations for the first time. The power of the Holy Spirit would fill the place where I was speaking. He sent healing and deliverance upon the people to confirm the teaching of the Word. (Mark 16:20) No matter how amazing the message was, or the signs and wonders that followed it, I still needed a hug from my Savior.

While worshipping the Lord one evening service I heard these words in my heart, "Come back to your first love." I felt an old feeling. As a young teenager, I was burning for God. I could not wait to get back to church every week to encounter God's presence! It was my LIFE. I would fight to go when I didn't feel well. I would participate in anything and everything I could just to encounter the presence of the Holy Spirit. He was and still is all I want. I pray for those who are lukewarm in the churches today, people who are okay without the gifts of the Holy Spirit. Once I tasted and saw that the Lord was good, there was no way I could ever go back!

These were the years of my youth, and that same overwhelming feeling once again consumed me as I stood praising God in that evening service.

I cried as I felt the personal side of the Lord for the first time in a long time. He spoke again to my heart and said, "I have put My Spirit on these services." Again, I had a flashback to my younger days in the church. I was attending a youth camp for about one week. The camp was awesome; swimming, basketball, boats, games, food, girls, and Holy Ghost meetings! I remember that Monday night the youth leader asked us to write down on a piece of paper what we wanted from God that week. As the offering bucket came by we were to toss in our paper and expect to receive from God what we had written down. I was so on fire, so in love with God, I had no idea what to write down. I eventually wrote **"more fire"** and put it in.

A few nights later in the Thursday evening meeting we were in intense praise and worship; however, this time it was not coming to an end. The band and singers just kept going. I looked around and most of everyone was sitting on the floor passing notes. I got so angry. I thought they had no zeal, no drive, no desire - no true love for the One who gave everything for us! This fired me up enough to keep standing with my hands raised and my eyes closed. I called it perseverance. Then came a "suddenly" moment! As clearly as I had just seen my peers passing notes, I suddenly saw the Gates of Heaven open above me! A large hand was directly behind the gates holding an enormous fire ball. The hand went back, poised to throw it towards me, like a baseball pitcher getting ready to throw a strike. I watched as the ball of fire flew from the Gates of Heaven all the way down until it hit me right in my belly. I physically felt it go inside of my spirit, and simultaneously my body got thrown back two rows of chairs! God blasted that place and it looked like a bomb had just hit.

There were several witnesses of what happened next. I began to roll in the Spirit. I rolled one way then turned, rolled the other way then turned, and rolled back to where I was sitting and never hit a wall or chair! That experience will continue to impact me for eternity. God answered the request on that piece of paper, and to this day the fire of God inside of me is uncontrollable!

Even with everything that was happening on the outside, those manifestations could never express what was happening in my heart and in my spirit. It was in these moments of my life that I connected with the God of the universe, spirit to Spirit. I would read the Bible and weep, the Word was too alive to handle with dignity. Everything in my life disappeared but Jesus. I could not wait to get alone so that I could hear His CURRENT VOICE! What is He saying right now? Not just a word or a revelation, but in that very moment where He is, what is He saying? I was head over heels in love, and there was nothing that could be done.

I believe we need to stop reading the Word to prove a point or make a statement, or say why someone is right or wrong. We need to get lost in the presence of our first love; it's the only way to truly KNOW the Word.

Revelation 2:2-5 (NKJV)
2
"I know your works, your labor, your patience, and that you cannot bear those who are evil. And you have tested those who say they are apostles and are not, and have found them liars;

THE ETERNAL PURPOSE OF MANKIND

3

and you have persevered and have patience, and have labored for My name's sake and have not become weary.

4

Nevertheless I have this against you, that you have left your first love.

5

Remember therefore from where you have fallen; repent and do the first works, or else I will come to you quickly and remove your lampstand from its place—unless you repent.

The fruits of the Spirit were developed and sin was hated, but it became only a religious practice of truth. They began to miss the intimacy with the Father. **Relationship without truth is just as worthless as truth without relationship.** My prayer is that we have both to the fullest.

1 John 4:19 (NKJV)
We love Him because He first loved us.

God is our first love. If we can't get alone to experience His love FIRST, then our actions, our fruit, and our hate for sin will all flow out of us without the Spirit of the living God, and without genuine love. So many believers seem to know very little about God. Why? They hear good sermons, help lead worship, volunteer in the children's church, and things of that nature. But without a true love encounter, it is just religious practice. That experience with the fireball is something that changed me; it was an encounter with the love of God that changed our relationship forever. Religious practice will not get you to really know someone; it won't get you to know God. Get alone with God and press into worship and relationship with Him. *Ask Him* to encounter you like He did for me and so many others. He's longing to change your life! Around the time that my first love with God was rekindled, I had a dream. I dreamed that I was in a church that I didn't recognize. I was singing to God with about a hundred other people, but I was very troubled in my heart. I could not sense His presence anywhere! Most of the dream had me frustrated trying to worship Him. I couldn't take it anymore; I SCREAMED from my heart and fell to my knees crying, "I repent! I repent!" Real tears soaked my actual pillow as I woke up in a kind of panic, still yelling. The Holy Spirit spoke to me as I became calm and laid back down. He said, "Your repentance is that of Revelation Chapter Two, and I'm calling you back to your first love."

__Philippians 3:2-10 (NKJV)__
2
Beware of dogs, beware of evil workers, beware of the mutilation!
3 For we are the circumcision, who worship God in the Spirit, rejoice in Christ Jesus, and __have no confidence in the flesh__,
4
though I also might have confidence in the flesh. If anyone else thinks he may have confidence in the flesh, I more so:
5
circumcised the eighth day, of the stock of Israel, of the tribe of Benjamin, a Hebrew of the Hebrews; concerning the law, a Pharisee;
6
concerning zeal, persecuting the church; concerning the righteousness which is in the law, blameless.

7
But what things were gain to me, these I have counted loss for Christ.
8
Yet indeed I also count all things loss for the excellence of the knowledge of Christ Jesus my Lord, for whom I have suffered the loss of all things, and count them as rubbish, that I may gain Christ
9
and be found in Him, not having my own righteousness, which is from the law, but that which is through faith in Christ, the righteousness which is from God by faith;
10
that I may know Him *and the power of His resurrection, and the fellowship of His sufferings, being conformed to His death,*

We are to have zero confidence in our flesh. We are to have zero confidence in our own works, in our church attendance, in knowing Greek and Hebrew meanings, in *anything* done in our own strength. All of my gain, my righteousness, my pride, my humility, my giving, my right living - all of it is nothing but LOSS! **I count all of this as loss that I may know Him.** This is referring to eternal life, not the length of years but the *quality* of life. To know the eternal God is eternal life. I want to know Him more than the reassurance of anything else I know, have done, or will do.

Philippians 3:18-20 (NKJV)
18
*For many walk, of whom I have told you often, **and now tell you even weeping,***

that they are the enemies of the cross of
Christ:
19
whose end is destruction, whose god is
their belly, and whose glory is in their
shame—who set their mind on earthly
things.
20
For our citizenship is in heaven, from which
we also eagerly wait for the Savior, the
Lord Jesus Christ,

The Holy Spirit revealed that my weeping in the dream was the same weeping from this passage. Weeping in repentance for trusting in earthly things, in our knowledge of the Bible, in our volunteering and random acts of kindness, in how we raise our families, and so on. Thank God our citizenship is in heaven! I challenge you to stop reading and find a place alone, with no music, TV, or cell phone. Be with your God! As you get to know Him, He will encounter you. Many who are reading this book will begin to have dreams, visions, and encounters from the Father, Jesus, and the Holy Spirit. You will never be the same!

CHAPTER ELEVEN

HUNGER

__Proverbs 27:20 (NKJV)__
Hell and Destruction are never full; So the eyes of man are never satisfied.

Our flesh is never satisfied, no matter how much we **FEED** it. I can eat and eat until I'm stuffed, but a few hours later I want some more. Every person I've ever met has self-control; they have it to whatever degree that they choose to have it. Some have self-control in the areas of sex, money, power, and so on. Others do not. Sometimes an individual is just "HUNGRY" enough to go and meet another woman while his wife sits at home with his children. **Hunger is a powerful, driving force.**

__Proverbs 26:11 (NKJV)__
As a dog returns to his own vomit, So a fool repeats his folly.

A fool will eat of the flesh and therefore throw it up, and out of **his intense hunger** will again eat what he just spewed up. A fool will not learn from his mistakes and be driven again into the same sins because he will not deny the hunger of his flesh.

Matthew 4:1-3 (NKJV)

1

Then Jesus was led up by the Spirit into the wilderness to be tempted by the devil.

2

*And when **He had fasted forty days and forty nights, afterward He was hungry.***

3

Now when the tempter came to Him, he said, "If You are the Son of God, command that these stones become bread."

One day in January I was sitting on my couch watching the snow fall, I began to think about this story. If someone we knew said that the Holy Spirit was leading them to go out into the woods for over a month without food, we would call that person "New Age," weird or crazy. We would say they were taking things too far, that they were lacking common sense and spiritual wisdom! It just kept hitting me. The Holy Spirit was the one who led Jesus to do this crazy fast!

Romans 8:14 (NKJV)

For as many as are led by the Spirit of God, these are sons of God.

Does God know more than us? Did Jesus know that by starving His flesh it would benefit Him in His spirit, soul, and body? Did Jesus need to fast to be able to handle the temptation from the devil? I would say yes to all three of these questions. Jesus was not tempted until after He was done fasting. **The fasting was preparation for the temptation.**

<u>Matthew 17:14-21 (NKJV)</u>

14

And when they had come to the multitude, a man came to Him, kneeling down to Him and saying,

15

"Lord, have mercy on my son, for he is an epileptic and suffers severely; for he often falls into the fire and often into the water.

16

So I brought him to Your disciples, but they could not cure him."

17

Then Jesus answered and said, "O faithless and perverse generation, how long shall I be with you? How long shall I bear with you? Bring him here to Me."

18

And Jesus rebuked the demon, and it came out of him; and the child was cured from that very hour.

19

Then the disciples came to Jesus privately and said, "Why could we not cast it out?"

20

*So Jesus said to them, "**Because of your unbelief**; for assuredly, I say to you, if you have faith as a mustard seed, you will say to this mountain, 'Move from here to there,' and it will move; and nothing will be impossible for you.*

21

*However, **this kind does not go out except by prayer and fasting."***

Why couldn't the disciples cast the demon out of the boy? Jesus said it was because of unbelief; they did not have the faith to deliver him. **Their faith was directly related to fasting and praying;** it was directly related to the "exchange table" and relationship. However, the fasting is first and then the praying/relationship. It is not a work that must be done for the Spirit of God to move in our lives; it is something that feeds our faith and makes us more aware of God and his victory than ourselves and our circumstances. For you and me to have a healthy relationship with God (who is Spirit), we must lessen our relationship with our flesh!

There are a lot of ways to decrease in the relationship that we have with ourselves, but scripturally, fasting is actually the best way. Some Christians run scared with their hands over their ears when this truth is brought up! I have met so many awesome people who believe that the teaching of fasting is controlling or law based, but they are just looking through the lens of law to begin with. **Religion will always try to say that there are many paths to God and His way of doing things, that way you will never offend anyone.** However, I am not scared to say that God is into the details, too. There is only one door to heaven and that is through Jesus Christ! There is a specific method that diminishes our relationship with our flesh and strengthens our relationship with the Father, and that is fasting. Not just fasting anything we pick, but actually fasting food. I am not against fasting social media, or fasting shopping or these kinds of things. However, that is a man-made fast and does not contain the power that fasting food for a period of time contains.

There are four men in the Bible who fasted for forty days that we know of. Moses actually fasted for forty days twice. The others include Jesus, Joshua, and Elijah. In the book of Exodus fasting is linked with closeness to the Father. The face of Moses beamed with the very glory of God! This is a great representation of becoming God's glory by getting on the cross and exchanging at God's table.

"Hunger always leaves after a few days of fasting and returns after a long fast – about 40 days – or when all toxins have been expelled from the body. One's breath then becomes as sweet as a baby's. Any normal healthy person can fast this long without harm. Starvation only begins after hunger returns. One must drink water during a long fast and break the fast gradually."

- Finis Dake

Health experts say that fasting for thirty days will break addictions of the flesh faster and healthier than any other method. This includes drinking, drugs, and smoking, among other things. They claim it will cleanse your entire body and heal almost all sickness and disease. The list includes, but is not limited to: high blood pressure, heart disease, skin ailments, and digestive issues.

Too many times we over-spiritualize being spiritual. We fall into the trap that nothing physical (other than sin) affects our walk with God. Remember, we are made out of this physical earth! (Isaiah 58:6-8, Psalm 35:13)

When I'm physically hungry my flesh is LOUDER than my spiritual hunger. It is only when I fast and I physically stop being hungry (it doesn't go away long enough when I'm eating because the flesh is never satisfied) that I can hear the true HUNGER of my Spirit! In those moments our flesh is not dominating all of our hunger!

John 4:31-34 (NKJV)
31
In the meantime His disciples urged Him, saying, "Rabbi, eat."
32
But He said to them, "I have food to eat of which you do not know."
33
Therefore the disciples said to one another, "Has anyone brought Him anything to eat?"
34
Jesus said to them, "My food is to do the will of Him who sent Me, and to finish His work.

I love that passage! After fasting for forty days, Jesus had a constant HUNGER for God's WILL in His life! The fasting of physical food created the intense spiritual hunger to do His Father's will and to finish His work. **Jesus exchanged natural hunger for spiritual hunger.**

Jesus overcame temptation in the wilderness and in the garden before His betrayal by the power of fasting! A lifestyle of fasting was punctuated by the intimate relationship with the Father in prayer in the garden. It caused Jesus to be hungry enough to do the will of His Father instead of His own. I believe God is calling His Body into a lifestyle of fasting FOOD again. There are some people without a strong enough hunger to do the Father's will. They have practiced feeding only the hunger of their flesh, and practice has made perfect. **Our hunger for God and to do His will is based upon quieting the hunger of our flesh.** Are you hungry enough?

I must pause right here and address works over the voice of the Holy Spirit. Fasting is not a work. Fasting is not law. Fasting is a very effective way to quiet the voice of our flesh and better hear the voice of our Father. **The BEST time to fast is when the Holy Spirit leads you to do so.** Remember, the Holy Spirit will not HURT YOU! If you are a beginner in the area of fasting, please get advice from your local pastor and fast in a healthy manner for your body. A lifestyle of fasting does not need to continually be forty days at a time. A lifestyle can be one day a week or even a month.

With that said, God spoke to me in January of 2014. **He said, "Fasting releases toxins, not just the toxins in your physical body but also in My Body**. When toxins begin to come out it will cause the body to smell and look unhealthy for a moment. There are toxins that have been a part of My Body, but as you fast they are leaving."

We had some toxins in our local Body at that time, and they had been there for years. After the Holy Spirit told me that fasting would remove the toxins, our entire leadership fasted food for about three to five days. Within fifteen days all of the toxins had left and the local Body began to mend and become whole and healthy again!

Did you know that fasting by faith will work to remove toxic relationships in your very own life? Those who will keep you from walking in your divine destiny? Fasting cuts through the flesh and goes right to the heart! It will open up the eyes of your spirit and lead you into being who you really are, and help you make decisions by the wisdom of God. I challenge you to begin a healthy lifestyle of fasting with the support of your pastors and spiritual leaders.

CHAPTER TWELVE

THE GARDEN SEASON

One thing many of us do not consider is that one right decision can change the course of our destiny. Of course the same thing is true of one bad decision. Our decisions and choices open and close doors along our journey into our destiny. It is entirely in our hands.

Luke 22:39-47 (NKJV)
39
Coming out, He went to the Mount of Olives, as He was accustomed, and His disciples also followed Him.
40
When He came to the place, **He said to them, "Pray that you may not enter into temptation."**
41
And He was withdrawn from them about a stone's throw, *and He knelt down and prayed,*
42
saying, "Father, if it is Your will, take this cup away from Me; nevertheless not My will, but Yours, be done."
43
Then an angel appeared to Him from heaven, strengthening Him.

THE ETERNAL PURPOSE OF MANKIND

44

And being in agony, He prayed more earnestly. Then His sweat became like great drops of blood falling down to the ground.

45

When He rose up from prayer, and had come to His disciples, He found them sleeping from sorrow.

46

Then He said to them, "Why do you sleep? Rise and pray, lest you enter into temptation."

Betrayal and Arrest in Gethsemane

47

And while He was still speaking, behold, a multitude; and he who was called Judas, one of the twelve, went before them and drew near to Jesus to kiss Him.

They were all in the same vicinity praying. They were all in the garden, and Jesus was right there with them. The disciples were praying to not ENTER into the realm of disobedience through temptation. **We need to pray and ask the Father what His will is in contrast to our own will just to know what to choose.** Will I obey Him or disobey Him? First, I need to know what He is really saying to me! One reason we sometimes struggle with obedience is because we think that our opinion is God's opinion. Many people do not ask God what He thinks or what He desires. Very few people purposefully choose to live in disobedience, but most people simply haven't asked to know the difference!

When we are in the "garden season" of our own lives, we will need extra strength like Jesus did before we can walk into our destiny. Jesus felt more frustration and more agony than ever before while the angel was strengthening Him in the garden! Many times we do not realize that God has sent angels to strengthen and encourage us in a time that seems like it might be the end. It feels like all hope is lost. Remember this account of Jesus in the garden; destiny is on the other side of this feeling! When we yield our hearts to the will of the Father, He will send us supernatural strength to get through the darkness!

The garden represents "knowing God." Jesus prayed and knew what His Father was telling Him. We are in a safe place while we find out what His will for us is. However, the garden feels unbearable. In the garden we will not just sweat, we will lose our own blood, a representation of losing our life for His life. It will be more intense than any trial we have ever had to go through. Toward the end of this season even your closest friends will have fallen asleep for sorrow, because the garden season for them was just too difficult. Many will lose their passion and fire in these times. You will feel alone, and other than God, you may truly be alone.

I believe Jesus is telling the sleepers in the garden to "WAKE UP," one more time. When the Spirit of God commands the Church to wake up it is not rude or harsh, it's needed for us to walk into our destiny. **When people who have been loyal to you begin to betray you and your obedience to the Father, know you are about to exit the garden!** To exit the garden is our desire; it is to walk into a destiny that will change the course of planet earth and the species of mankind forever. When Jesus left the garden season He walked into His destiny, to die upon the cross. That event changed the course of history forever!

You might be at a place where one decision will thrust you one way or another. Thank You Jesus for making the decision to submit to the Father's will. The garden season is the season in our lives to find out the Father's will. It is a season to be hungry enough to say yes to the Father's will. It is the season prior to walking into divine destiny. **It is a season of choice.**

Genesis 3:6-13 (NKJV)

6
So when the woman saw that the tree was good for food, that it was pleasant to the eyes, and a tree desirable to make one wise, she took of its fruit and ate. She also gave to her husband with her, and he ate.

7
Then the eyes of both of them were opened, and they knew that they were naked; and they sewed fig leaves together and made themselves coverings.

8
And they heard the sound of the Lord God walking in the garden in the cool of the day, and Adam and his wife hid themselves from the presence of the Lord God among the trees of the garden.

9
Then the Lord God called to Adam and said to him, "Where are you?"

10
So he said, "I heard Your voice in the garden, and I was afraid because I was naked; and I hid myself."

11
And He said, "Who told you that you

were naked? Have you eaten from the tree of which I commanded you that you should not eat?"

12

Then the man said, "The woman whom You gave to be with me, she gave me of the tree, and I ate."

13

And the Lord God said to the woman, "What is this you have done?" The woman said, "The serpent deceived me, and I ate."

In the garden, a different garden, Adam and Eve were tempted and they fell into disobedience. In the garden the disciples were told to pray so they would not fall into temptation. **Satan is lurking in the garden season of your life hoping to deceive you from exiting under the right decisions and walking into your divine destiny.** Adam and Eve heard God walking in the garden; they ran and hid from Him. They ran and hid based on feelings of condemnation, feelings that God was upset and displeased with them. These feelings will always lead into disobedience.

God asked them, "Who told you? Why are you believing Satan as if it is Me? Your knowledge is based off of lies that you are accepting because of how you feel about yourself. Come back and know Me. Let those feelings of deceit die."

The first Adam failed the garden season and never stepped into mankind's divine destiny. It was everyone's fault except their own. Bitterness, resentment, unworthiness, and frustration flooded them in the garden. **It wasn't the garden's fault, it wasn't God's fault, but it was a heart issue with them!** Thank God we have the second Adam (Jesus) replacing us in this vessel! I challenge you to submit to the Father in the garden season. You might lose some sleep, sweat, and blood. You might have to suffer persecution to fully submit to the Father's will. The persecution might be from your husband, wife, parents, children, friends, or co-workers. I dare you to exit that garden in the Father's will and walk right into a history altering destiny!

CHAPTER THIRTEEN

LEAVING WITH JOY

Matthew 14:22-33 (NKJV)

22

Immediately Jesus made His disciples get into the boat and go before Him to the other side, while He sent the multitudes away.

23

And when He had sent the multitudes away, He went up on the mountain by Himself to pray. Now when evening came, He was alone there.

24

But the boat was now in the middle of the sea, tossed by the waves, for the wind was contrary.

25

Now in the fourth watch of the night Jesus went to them, walking on the sea.

26

And when the disciples saw Him walking on the sea, they were troubled, saying, "It is a ghost!" And they cried out for fear.

27

*But **immediately Jesus spoke to them, saying, "Be of good cheer! It is I; do not be afraid."***

28

And Peter answered Him and said, "Lord, if it is You, command me to come to You on the water."

29

*So He said, "Come." And **when Peter had come down out of the boat, he walked on the water to go to Jesus.***

30

But when he saw that the wind was boisterous, he was afraid; and beginning to sink he cried out, saying, "Lord, save me!"

31

And immediately Jesus stretched out His hand and caught him, and said to him, "O you of little faith, why did you doubt?"

32

And when they got into the boat, the wind ceased.

33

Then those who were in the boat came and worshiped Him, saying, "Truly You are the Son of God."

Again, we see Jesus has gone on alone to pray, to know the Father. At three a.m. He came back walking on the water. Jesus comes to us to call us into our destiny at the heights of our trials and tribulations. The disciples were filled with anxiety and began to panic. They became overwhelmed with fear just as Jesus, their strength, was showing up. In the same way, Jesus had become overwhelmed with agony before the angel came on the scene to strengthen Him in the garden. Many times we will feel overwhelmed and frustrated while we are being strengthened. However, in those times, if we are not being strengthened by the Lord, our own strength will not be enough. How many times has His strength pulled us through, and we didn't even know it?

The first thing Jesus said to them was, "You! Let fear die and cheer up!" Peter was the only one who reacted out of his heart and not from his flesh and emotions. Many times our feelings or even what is convenient in the moment dictates how we react to God. What would the Church look like if she reacted from her heart to what God says? Peter clung to Jesus! He clung to joy and faith more than to frustration and fear! **Faith does not work without joy!**

Peter didn't NEED Jesus to help him. Peter needed to remain clinging to his joy and faith. The issue was that Peter began to focus on frustration and fear. Frustration is like complaining; it will prevent us from entering into the promise land! We want to end up like Jesus. We want to be the ones outside of the boat, walking through the storm in perfect peace, helping those who are sinking to continue standing!

Peter walked out of the boat (a garden season) by keeping his focus on Jesus, joy, and faith. Boats also symbolically represent ministry. **I believe many ministers and disciples of Christ need to step out of the religious confines of man-made ministry and "walk on water" into their destiny!**

James 1:2-4 (NKJV)
2
My brethren, count it all joy when you fall into various trials,

3

*knowing that the testing of your faith
produces patience.*

4

*But let patience have its perfect work, that
you may be perfect and complete, lacking
nothing.*

Are we to count it all frustration? Regard it all as pain? NO! Rejoice! According to this passage faith is actually counting the trial as joy! Jesus told Peter to rejoice. Once Peter stopped rejoicing and began to sink, Jesus said, "You have LITTLE faith." **When we refuse to rejoice we have more faith in our circumstance and frustrations than we do in God.**

Hebrews 12:1-2 (NKJV)

1

*Therefore we also, since we are surrounded
by so great a cloud of witnesses, let us lay
aside every weight, and the sin which so
easily ensnares us, and let us run with
endurance the race that is set before us,*

2

***looking unto Jesus, the author and
finisher of our faith, who for the joy that
was set before Him endured the cross,*** *despising the shame, and has sat down at
the right hand of the throne of God.*

How did Jesus have the faith to endure the cross while exiting the garden season? He took the JOY set before Him by faith! **Joy was the strategy the angel brought to strengthen Jesus!** Without that joy, Jesus would have never left the garden and never fulfilled His destiny. We become the fruit of the cross when faith and joy are produced in us. We become like Him. We walk into our destiny. We cannot get upon that wooden cross, let the tree grow and become the fruit of the cross without joy and rejoicing in the garden! The children of Israel complained; they remained frustrated in the wilderness. They did not rejoice, and they did not enter into the promised land. They did not fulfill their destiny. **You may still be in the garden, but the choice to make is the choice of joy.**

Isaiah 55:8-13 (NKJV)

8
"For My thoughts are not your thoughts, Nor are your ways My ways," says the Lord.

9
"For as the heavens are higher than the earth, So are My ways higher than your ways, And My thoughts than your thoughts.

10
"For as the rain comes down, and the snow from heaven, And do not return there, But water the earth, And make it bring forth and bud, That it may give seed to the sower And bread to the eater,

11
So shall My word be that goes forth from My mouth; It shall not return to Me void, But it shall accomplish what I please, And it shall prosper in the thing for which I sent it.

12
"For you shall go out with joy, And be led out with peace; The mountains and the hills Shall break forth into singing before you, And all the trees of the field shall clap their hands.

13
Instead of the thorn shall come up the cypress
tree, And instead of the brier shall come up
the myrtle tree; And it shall be to the Lord for
a name, For an everlasting sign that shall not
be cut off."

The word of God shall prosper in the thing in which it was
sent. God is saying that what He SAYS will prosper in the
divine destiny that He gave it to accomplish! How will it
prosper? **You shall go out with JOY!** You shall go out of
the garden with the joy set before you. Peter walked on
water by joy. Jesus went to the cross by joy. The garden
season can get people to look inward and begin to have self-
pity. I challenge you to run from self-pity, run from being
overly frustrated, and exit the garden by counting all the trials
and persecutions as joy.

CHAPTER FOURTEEN

ENJOY THE NOW

You have an amazing destiny to fulfill. You are created in God's image and likeness for the purpose of humiliating the devil. You are loved by the Father, and are becoming one with the Holy Trinity. There is divine purpose for the human race, and divine purpose for each individual. These truths have burned in my spirit for many years. As I continue to walk into my divine destiny, I stumble sometimes in knowing what to do NEXT. Have you ever been there? In prayer one day I asked the Lord, "What do you want me to do right now, as I continue to believe and walk with you?" I had so many prophetic words over my life, my family's life, and the ministry. I thought there was a way I could help those words come to pass faster.

The Father answered me, "Get lost in the moment, as if there are no time constraints. Begin to live like Jesus did. He followed the guideline of time to follow My will, but in His heart and soul (emotions) He allowed time to stop; He lived outside of time." That was not the answer I was expecting to hear! I thought He would tell me to pray more, or to rally the troops and get something done. It took time, but I slowly began to understand that RIGHT NOW God has blessed me as much as in what is to come. I'm not striving to become what I already am, and neither are you! God tells us that we are righteous; we do not have to work to please God for acceptance. We do not always feel righteous, but it is who we are, even right now! We are who God says we are, and we have what God says we have! His WORD, His voice is the final authority in our lives. We need to get out of the mindset of I see myself "here" instead of "there." I challenge you to never speak who you or anyone else says you are, but only speak who God says you are!

> ### Matthew 6:24 (NKJV)
> *"No one can serve two masters; for either he will hate the one and love the other, or else he will be loyal to the one and despise the other. You cannot serve God and mammon.*

> ### Matthew 6:33-34 (NKJV)
> *33*
> *But **seek first the kingdom of God and His righteousness, and all these things shall be added to you**.*
> *34*
> *Therefore do not worry about tomorrow, for tomorrow will worry about its own things. Sufficient for the day is its own trouble.*

We either serve God as Lord or mammon as Lord. When mammon is our Lord it **produces worry** because mammon is a substance or system and not a person who we can rely upon. Jesus is *a person t*hat we can rely upon! Therefore seek God as Lord and *you* will become Lord over the mammon! You and I have the ability to not worry, if we seek the right Lord. Worry is fear of the future or the unknown, and in regard to this **we need to live in today!**

To be Lord means to have power and authority. Whoever is our Lord has power and authority over us. I do not want mammon or money to have authority over me! We choose who our Lord will be. (Joshua 24:13-15) We choose who will rule over us. Everyone submits. The question is, to whom do you submit? Some submit to bitterness and unforgiveness, others submit to joy and peace. WE have the choice to submit to mammon or to God.

> ### _John 16:33 (NKJV)_
> _These things I have spoken to you, that in Me you may have peace. In the world you will have tribulation; but be of good cheer, I have overcome the world."_

In this life there will be trouble, **so cheer up IN THE MOMENT!** We need to quit trying to make something happen in a troubled world and allow God to make it happen while we're in peace RIGHT NOW. Faith is not something you have to pedal faster to get to work. Faith is not a work. Faith can be very quiet and peaceful. Jesus had more faith than all of the disciples while He was sleeping in the boat, not doing anything. With all the effort and work we put into things, there is a good chance we will get somewhere or get something accomplished, but it may not be what God has promised you. It may not be divine destiny. There are a lot of choices we can make every day. Which ones do we make? I found out that if we follow the voice of the Holy Spirit, He will guide us into the right choices without us having to be overworked.

After Adam and Eve had sinned, God came walking (not screaming in rage), into the garden. He was looking for them in that moment. However, Adam and Eve lived in the condemnation of the past. They were worried what their future now held since they had failed. They were unsure, even though

God was acting like nothing had happened. Most of us live in fast-forward or in re-wind. *What would it look like to allow the goodness of God to take Lordship right now?* People have missed many things in life because of the overwhelming worry of their past mistakes and failures, while contemplating how it will affect their future. But now is the precious time where you and I can do whatever we want to do! **Living in the now requires one thing of us - trust in God as Lord.**

I love food. Have you ever been around people who condemn themselves for every little bite of pizza they take? They are not enjoying the moment! If we are going to choose to eat pizza we should ENJOY every single bite we take! If we choose to abstain from pizza, let us enjoy that, too!

Romans 14:22-23 (NKJV)
22
Do you have faith? Have it to yourself before God. Happy is he who does not condemn himself in what he approves.
23
*But he who doubts is condemned if he eats, because he does not eat from faith; for **whatever is not from faith is sin**.*

Worry negates the faith that you have in God and in yourself. Our doubt in every choice that we make destroys living and enjoying the moment! As you have confidence in the choices that you make in faith, do not allow anyone else to condemn you, judge you, and bring you down.

Isaiah 54:17 (NKJV)
*No **weapon** formed against you shall prosper, And **every tongue** which rises against you in judgment You shall*

condemn. This is the heritage of the servants of the Lord, And their righteousness is from Me, "Says the Lord.

What are the weapons here? Voices rising up in judgement and condemnation! To trust God and enjoy the moment we will need to condemn the negative words in our lives. Do not allow words to RULE over you. Do not allow any word other than God's Word to Lord over your life!

Psalm 27:13-14 (NKJV)
13
I would have lost heart, unless I had believed That I would see the goodness of the Lord In the land of the living.
14
Wait on the Lord; Be of good courage, And He shall strengthen your heart; Wait, I say, on the Lord!

Believers can fall into the trap that nothing matters on this side of heaven, so to speak. This trap prevents us from enjoying the moment and watching God win the battles for us right now. God has something good for each of us in these very moments. David said that he would have lost heart, lost hope, if he did not believe that God was going to bless him now, on this earth. What would it be like to walk in the now and let God go before us and take the land? We would *walk* into blessings instead of *striving* after them. We would stumble into victories without having fought for them. We could sleep in the storm and laugh in the face of calamity.

DOMINION

CHAPTER FIFTEEN

FAR ABOVE

> ### Genesis 1:26-28 (NKJV)
>
> **26**
>
> *Then God said, "Let Us make man in Our image, according to Our likeness; **let them have dominion** over the fish of the sea, over the birds of the air, and over the cattle, over all[a] the earth and over every creeping thing that creeps on the earth."*
>
> **27**
>
> *So God created man in His own image; in the image of God He created him; male and female He created them.*
>
> **28**
>
> *Then **God blessed them**, and God said to them, "Be fruitful and multiply; fill the earth and subdue it; **have dominion** over the fish of the sea, over the birds of the air, and over every living thing that moves on the earth."*

The word dominion is only used for God and mankind in the Bible. **One cannot have dominion power over something or someone without the ability to do everything that the subjects of their dominion can do.** You may want to re-read that last line! This strongly implies that mankind could have flown before the fall, and swam as deep as the fish. We already discussed how mankind has dominion over the sun, moon, and stars. Where are the sun, moon, and stars located? In the heavenlies!

> ### *Ephesians 1:20-23 (NKJV)*
> **20**
> *which He worked in Christ when He raised Him from the dead and seated Him at His right hand **in the heavenly places,***
> **21**
> ***far above** all principality and power and might and **dominion**, and every name that is named, not only in this age but also in that which is to come.*
> **22**
> *And He put all things under His feet, and gave Him to be head over all things to the church,*
> **23**
> *which is His body, the fullness of Him who fills all in all.*

> ### *Ephesians 2:6-7 (NKJV)*
> **6**
> *and **raised us up together, and made us sit together in the heavenly places in Christ Jesus,***
> **7**
> *that in the ages to come He might show the exceeding riches of His grace in His kindness toward us in Christ Jesus.*

We have been raised with Christ FAR ABOVE dominion in the heavenly places! Jesus redeemed us back to the garden, but even HIGHER! In the fall, mankind (Adam and Eve) gave "the heavenlies" over to Satan and demons, because that is where dominion rules from. However, Jesus came and raised us FAR ABOVE the dominion in the heavenlies, to the full authority of God Himself. This is why Satan could tempt Jesus with the kingdoms of this earth in the fourth chapter of Luke. Satan had dominion over all of the kingdoms and governments of the earth. However, Jesus came and disarmed Satan, or stripped him of his dominion!

Colossians 2:15 (NKJV)
Having disarmed principalities and powers, He made a public spectacle of them, triumphing over them in it.

To those who believe we are FAR ABOVE, we have full authority and dominion. To those who do not believe, they still submit to the demons in the heavenlies. 1 John 5:19 declares that the whole world lies under the sway of the wicked one. We who believe are no longer of the world though we are in it; our citizenship is from heaven!
Because we are seated in the heavenlies far above the deceptive authority of the devil, our spirit is in the throne room of God as much as it is in our physical bodies.

Hebrews 4:14-16 (NKJV)
14
*Seeing then that we have a great High Priest **who has passed through the heavens**, Jesus the Son of God, let us hold fast our confession.*
15
For we do not have a High Priest who cannot sympathize with our weaknesses, but was in all points tempted as we are, yet without sin.

16
Let us therefore come boldly to the throne
of grace, that we may obtain mercy and
*find grace to **help in time of need**.*

Jesus passed through the dominion of the heavenlies! Hold fast to your confession! How do we come boldly to the throne room? We come boldly by speaking or agreeing, that we, the real us, are already there whenever we need Him! **In a time of need we can move from an earthly encounter to a heavenly encounter!** Paul did it! Stephen did it! Stephen said He looked and saw an open heaven with Jesus standing at the right hand of the Father. Stephen simply went right from earth straight to the throne room! (Acts 7:56-60)

Matthew 28:18-20 (NKJV)
18
And Jesus came and spoke to them, saying,
*"**All authority** has been given to Me in*
heaven and on earth.
19
__Go therefore__ and make disciples of all the
nations, baptizing them in the name of the
Father and of the Son and of the Holy
Spirit,
20
teaching them to observe all things that I
have commanded you; and lo, I am with
you always, even to the end of the age."
Amen.

Jesus has given all authority and dominion to mankind in heaven and on earth, in two places! Two represents unity; this is divine unity between God and man. Go to all nations, all kingdoms, all governments and invade! Bring the Kingdom of God back to this land!

CHAPTER SIXTEEN

BEFORE THEIR TIME

We will begin this chapter by drawing our attention to the story of Daniel. I'd like to focus in on the point in time when Daniel had already been made a ruler over the whole province of Babylon because of his supernatural interpretation of King Nebuchadnezzar's dreams. This is after the story of Shadrack, Meshack, and Abednigo and the miracle at the fiery furnace. At this point in our story Darius is the king.

Daniel 6:3-5 (NKJV)

3

Then this Daniel distinguished himself above the governors and satraps, because an excellent spirit was in him; and the king gave thought to setting him over the whole realm.

4

So the governors and satraps sought to find some charge against Daniel concerning the kingdom; but they could find no charge or fault, because he was faithful; nor was there any error or fault found in him.

5

Then these men said, "We shall not find any charge against this Daniel unless we find it against him concerning the law of his God."

Daniel 6:14-15 (NKJV)

14
And the king, when he heard these words, was greatly displeased with himself, and set his heart on Daniel to deliver him; and he labored till the going down of the sun to deliver him.
15
Then these men approached the king, and said to the king, "Know, O king, that it is the law of the Medes and Persians that no decree or statute which the king establishes may be changed."

I want to use this story in Daniel to encourage you. Even when it looks like you have a huge setback, you still have full dominion. The first thing to notice is that while God begins to bless and prosper you into your divine destiny, there will be those who will manipulate others around them to harm you or your reputation in some way. This is only due to an ever growing jealousy within them. I have never seen a servant of God truly prosper without attacks and lashing out from some of those who used to be on the same level as them. The second thing to notice is that the king was *for Daniel.* **There will be those who are for you, but may have no choice but to fail you.** The reason is so that God will end up receiving all the glory in your life. Do not find it strange when those who are really for you cannot do anything to help you.

Daniel 6:16-17 (NKJV)

16
So the king gave the command, and they

*brought Daniel and cast him into the den
of lions. But the king spoke, saying to
Daniel, "Your God, whom you serve
continually, He will deliver you."*
17
*Then a stone was brought and laid on the
mouth of the den, and the king sealed it
with his own signet ring and with the
signets of his lords, that the purpose
concerning Daniel might not be changed.*

The third thing to notice is the lions. The lions were the "right now" problem for Daniel; it was what was staring him right in the face. The devil may have deceitfully plotted against you. He may have turned those who were for you against you. Those friends of yours had to do the "right thing." All of this has led you to where you are now and what is staring you in the face - roaring lions.

1 Peter 5:5-10 (NKJV)
5
*Likewise you younger people, submit
yourselves to your elders. Yes, all of you
be submissive to one another, and be
clothed with humility, for "God resists the
proud, But gives grace to the humble."*
6
*Therefore humble yourselves under the
mighty hand of God, **that He may exalt
you in due time**, 7*
*casting all your care upon Him, for He
cares for you.*
8
*Be sober, be vigilant; because **your
adversary the devil walks about like a***

roaring lion, seeking whom he may devour.

9

Resist him, steadfast in the faith, knowing that the same sufferings are experienced by your brotherhood in the world.

10

But may the God of all grace, who called us[d] to His eternal glory by Christ Jesus, after you have suffered a while, perfect, establish, strengthen, and settle you.

God will exalt you in due season, so get rid of your worries and throw them upon Jesus. Why? Because the devil is like a roaring lion trying to devour you! Resist the devil in your faith; have faith in the power of the Blood of Jesus, and God will give you ALL the grace that you need! It doesn't matter what happened to get you to what is staring you in the face, **the devil is the guilty one!**

Daniel 6:20-23 (NKJV)

20

And when he came to the den, he cried out with a lamenting voice to Daniel. The king spoke, saying to Daniel, "Daniel, servant of the living God, has your God, whom you serve continually, been able to deliver you from the lions?"

21

Then Daniel said to the king, "O king, live forever!

22

My God sent His angel and shut the lions' mouths, so that they have not hurt me, because I was found innocent before

*Him; and also, O king, I have done no
wrong before you."*
23
*Now the king was exceedingly glad for
him, and commanded that they should take
Daniel up out of the den. So Daniel was
taken up out of the den, and no injury
whatever was found on him, because he
believed in his God.*

God did not actually send His angel to shut the lions'
mouths. The original word for "angel" here is the same as in
the story of Shadrack, Meshack, and Abednigo where one
was seen like the Son of Man standing in the furnace with
them! Daniel is saying that Jesus, the Son of God was in the
lion's den muzzling the mouths of the lions! Daniel said,
"Because I am innocent before Him." The H in "Him" is
capitalized. We are innocent before God because of the shed
Blood of Jesus Christ. **It was His Blood saving Daniel
from Satan's false accusations, coming as a roaring lion
long before Jesus came to this earth!** It is His Blood that
makes us innocent now, nullifying all the accusations against
us from the enemy in this day.

Daniel 6:24 (NKJV)
*And the king gave the command, and they
brought those men who had accused
Daniel, and they cast them into the den of
lions—them, their children, and their
wives; and the lions overpowered them,
and broke all their bones in pieces before
they ever came to the bottom of the den.*

Those who accuse you falsely and speak out against you,
though His Blood says you are forgiven and righteous, open

the door for Satan, the roaring lion, to come in to consume and devour. The plans of the devil are a trap for himself. Isaiah 54:17 says no weapon formed against us shall prosper. No weapon, no matter how deceitful the plotting may be. This was Daniel's heritage before Christ, and it is our heritage after Christ. Truthfully, those who come against us need our prayers! (Matthew 5:44)

> ### *Romans 16:20 (NKJV)*
> *And the God of peace **will crush** Satan under your feet shortly. The grace of our Lord Jesus Christ be with you. Amen.*

That word **crush** means to shatter and break bones. In the story of Daniel, the roaring lions break their bones BEFORE they even hit the bottom of the den! The bottom of the den is a representation of hell. Every plan Satan sets up for you is on its way to fail; it is doomed to the pit. Before your enemies can even set foot at the bottom of hell, Satan will crush their bones! Who devoured these enemies of Daniel BEFORE they hit the bottomless pit? The lions! The devil went to take your life, yet devoured your poverty instead. He went to consume you, but ate your failures instead. The enemies of God (sin, sickness, and poverty) were defeated at the cross! **I have good news for you, the devil will not take you out; he is devouring himself!**

All of the lions were in one place to consume Daniel, in the den. In Psalm 110:1 it declares, "*The Lord said to my Lord, "Sit at My right hand, Till I make Your enemies Your footstool."*" We are to rule in the midst of our enemies!

> ### *Revelation 12:10-11 (NKJV)*
> **10**
> *Then I heard a loud voice saying in heaven,*

"Now salvation, and strength, and the kingdom of our God, and the power of His Christ have come, for the accuser of our brethren, who accused them before our God day and night, has been cast down.
11
And they overcame him by the blood of the Lamb and by the word of their testimony, *and they did not love their lives to the death.*

The devil accuses us; we overcome by the Blood of Jesus Christ. I challenge you to begin to think of the devil as the guilty one. As long as you are covered by the Blood of Jesus you are no longer guilty and should stop entertaining the thoughts of overwhelming guilt. After you realize that you are covered by the Blood of Jesus you need to SAY IT! ("<u>and</u> by the WORD of their testimony")

His Blood crushed our enemies BEFORE their time! This is why we receive the Kingdom of God before it's physically here. We can receive the goodness of God before it is even time, by the Blood shed by Jesus since the foundation of man's world. Our dominion and authority as mankind can almost seem unreal, but it is our reality.

There are reputable miraculous reports of people flying, walking on water, being transported from city to city, and the like that aren't usually brought to the light in our church culture. This is besides the "common" miraculous testimonies happening constantly all over the world of supernatural healing, deliverance, raising of the dead, and the life abundant in Christ that turns His people's lives around. I pray this book is just the beginning of opening your heart and mind to who you really are in Christ Jesus. Kenneth E Hagin prophesied that the generation that ushered in the return of Jesus would be a generation that understood its true authority. This is just the beginning. There is so much more to discover in God's Word and in this earth. I challenge you to begin walking in dominion and authority on levels you have never dreamed of walking. The Holy Spirit is ready to back you up, to humiliate the devil and all his works, and to help you fulfill the divine destiny that has been birthed in your heart.

CONCLUSION

Not long before the Lord had impressed me to write this book, the Holy Spirit gave me a dream. I was walking toward a church in my city, and many hungry people were inside waiting for me to come in and minister to them. I paused for a moment and took the time to stop in a grassy area off to the side to change my shoes. They were a new pair of an old style of converse shoes, the same type of shoes I would have worn when I was younger. They were a sort of khaki cream color, something I feel like only I would choose. There are a lot more details in the dream, but I want to focus on the shoes.

God was showing me that I needed to put on the style of shoes that fit me. In the story of David and Goliath, David did not wear the armor that did not fit him. I have a divine purpose and destiny, and I cannot try to wear someone else's shoes. I must wear the style and fit that looks and feels good on me so I can walk forward into my purpose with confidence.

It was no coincidence that I worked at and managed a shoe store for almost seven years where it was my job to fit orthotics into a style that fit a particular individual. It was in the back of this shoe store where the Holy Spirit began to download this revelation to me.

In Ephesians 6:15 regarding the armor of God it states, *"and having shod your feet with the preparation of the*

THE ETERNAL PURPOSE OF MANKIND

gospel of peace;" This is referring to the ministry of reconciliation. The ministry of reconciliation is the purpose we all have as members of the Body of Christ, to reconcile the world to God! What shoes you wear has everything to do with your purpose. God was telling me not to get distracted, but to put on the shoes that fit me so I could walk out my divine purpose!

John 1:27 (NKJV)
It is He who, coming after me, is preferred before me, whose sandal strap I am not worthy to loose."

These were the words of John the Baptist. Jesus had the perfect fit to walk in His purpose on this earth, and this is why John the Baptist said, "I cannot untie His shoes"!

The human race has a united purpose in humiliating the devil. The next step is to discover your unique individual purpose, the shoe that fits.

God trained me for years in a real shoe store. I measured people's feet, measured their arch length, gave tips on plantar fasciitis, discerned orthotics, and bent down and fit the shoes to their specific feet. Now I help people find the right style and fit of shoe to walk out their divine call, destiny, and purpose. I help to equip the Body of Christ with what they might need if something has been hindering their walk and needs to be healed or adjusted.

This is why here in Carmel, Indiana, I was called to begin a ministerial school, **"The School of Moses"** under Turning Point Ministries, which we birthed after those years at the shoe store. In Deuteronomy chapter 8 and chapter 29, when the children of Israel were led out of Egypt (the world's system) by Moses, it says that their shoes did not even wear out! It is our purpose to empower you with your purpose! It is our purpose to lead God's people out of this world system way of doing things and into the Kingdom of God.

If you feel ready to move up to the next level in your life and begin to receive the equipping you need to propel you into your destiny and purpose, I challenge you to consider a school that will not just give you the knowledge of the Word with signs and wonders accompanying the teaching, but a school that makes its aim to put you in the shoes intended for you to walk out your individual and corporate purpose on this earth. Please visit our website for more information:

www.turningpointnorth.com

www.schoolofmoses.com

Together, as every joint supplies, we will put on the shoes that fit, preparing feet to bring the gospel around the world and walk out our divine purpose - giving glory to God, and humiliating the devil.

ABOUT THE AUTHOR

In 2009 Pastor David and his wife Jess began Turning Point Ministries in Carmel, Indiana, after graduating Rhema Bible College in 2005 under Kenneth E Hagin. They lead a strong, Spirit-filled church with love, compassion, and truth. In 2012 the Holy Spirit told Pastor Natali to start a Ministry School and said these words, "build a legacy." In 2015, the name of the school became the "School of Moses" by the inspiration of the Holy Spirit. Over two and a half million people were freed from slavery in the time of Moses. There are over seven billion people on the earth today. A mass exodus is needed in this time so there may be a generation that ushers in the return of our King! Many are being led to the School of Moses every year to be fitted into their divine purpose and call for this very reason.

Pastor Natali is set to continue the mission that Jesus told Kenneth E Hagin to do, "Go and teach My people faith!" Healings, miracles, signs, and wonders are being wrought by God in this ministry. God's people are being freed - the legacy is being built!

If you would like to contact the author, please write:

Turning Point Ministries
PO Box 3626
Carmel, IN 46082

or call: (317) 650-2188

on facebook:: Turning.point.north

on instagram: turningpointnorth/

on twitter: @turningpointnor

on the web: www.turningpointnorth.com

on the web: www.schoolofmoses.com

on youtube: Turningpoint north

Please include your testimony or help received from this book when you write.